SINFUL SOCIAL STRUCTURES

Sinful
Social Structures

by
Patrick Kerans

PAULIST PRESS
New York / Paramus / Toronto

Library of Congress
Catalog Card Number: 74-76716

ISBN: 0-8091-1830-0

Published by Paulist Press
Editorial Office: 1865 Broadway, N.Y., N.Y. 10023
Business Office: 400 Sette Drive, Paramus, N.J. 07652

Printed and bound in the
United States of America

Contents

PART I

SOCIETY'S NEED FOR A NOTION OF SIN AND FORGIVENESS

PART II

THE NOTION OF SOCIAL SIN

Editor's Foreword

Most of us think of sin in terms of personal, one-to-one relationships. Morality, for the majority of North American Christians, deals primarily with Fifth, Sixth and Seventh Commandment conduct. Adjunct concerns about the "Sunday obligation," reverence for God's name, telling the truth, etc., tend also to focus on the interpersonal area—God and I; you and I. This book puts that "you" in the plural number and shows how the sinful tendencies in the singular "I" (greed, lust, sloth and the other root tendencies toward sin) can be projected into sinful social structures, wherein "I" with other "I's" in a given society can sinfully damage a collection or community of "you's" who suffer various forms of oppression, exploitation and injustice.

To sketch this out in a small book is no easy task. Finding readers for such a book may not be a simple matter either. Most readers will want to dissociate themselves from what Patrick Kerans calls "social sin." The reader doesn't even know an Angolan coffee worker; how can he be guilty of sinning against him? Sure, you drink coffee and live well while he, in return for his coffee-producing effort, receives little pay and no hope for future security, but where does sin enter that particular picture? You are charitable and just to all the blacks you deal with; how can guilt for the social sin of racial prejudice or the systematic subordination of blacks be laid at your door? You stand (or sit) on the heavy side of the world's economic imbalance. Must you feel guilty, not only emotionally, but also morally, because you have more while others have less? Dr. Kerans would say that you should, at least to the extent that your prosperity is the cause of their poverty. In a general way, this book tries to measure that extent.

It is late, but not too late for Christians to examine their complicity in or with the forces of social evil in this world. This small book makes a positive contribution to that monumental task.

Sin, personal or social, is a mystery. " 'Sin' is a judgmental word," writes Dr. Kerans, "a word we use about a past decision from which we now dissociate ourselves. It *now* is seen to have been a senseless, destructive choice, even though *then* it seemed to have been perfectly reasonable. In confessing sin, a man tries to shine light on the darkness of that moment."

The author is a professional theologian and a trained economist. His effort is to shed light on a dark area to which theologians have only recently turned their attention. His book is brief and, therefore, easily reread, if not easily read on the first excursion through biblical, historical and social analyses of an issue that deserves every bit of the attention it is now receiving in the contemporary Christian consciousness.

Sinful Social Structures appears in the new Paulist Press series, "Topics in Moral Argument." Authors for this series are invited to argue a moral position. Readers are expected not to substitute an author's authority for their own personal and responsible decision-making. In the present instance, readers are invited to use this book to shine some light on the ethical darkness surrounding poverty and other contemporary social problems.

William J. Byron, S.J.
Loyola University, New Orleans

Introduction

We live in an age of unprecedented wealth, of un-dreamed of technical knowledge. But only a few people on this earth share these boons of modern industrialized society. Modern growth is good, but the resultant in-equality is, I submit, evil. It is evil in its consequences: it keeps the poorer majority from their fair share of this world's goods, and often from the bare necessities required to live decently; it leaves the rich minority (those earning over $3,000 a year) hollow and frustrat-ed by the rat-race of consumerism; it is, we have lately been finding out, seriously straining the ability of our environment to sustain life.

But *what kind of evil* is here involved? Is it one more example of the harshness of life? Is it simply the result of technical difficulties which, if we "do not ad-just our set," modern know-how will soon solve? Is it the institutional embodiment of moral evil, of sinful human decisions? No doubt each of these explanations has some truth to it. However, I am convinced that, in our technological society, most people are prone to see only technical problems when in reality many of our problems are the result of sin. Certainly there are no specifically Christian solutions to technical problems, but Christians can and ought to have much more to say about many of today's social crises, since they are the result of human sin.

In the fall of 1971, the Third Synod of Bishops met. One of the two themes discussed was international justice. In the Synod text later endorsed by Pope Paul VI and entitled "Justice in the World," we read: ". . . we have . . . been able to perceive the serious injustices which are building around the world a *network* of domination, oppression and abuses which stifle freedom."[1]

The Bishops describe themselves as having listened to those "who suffer violence and are oppressed by *unjust systems and structures*." They speak of the Church's mission for the redemption of the human race and its "liberation from every *oppressive situation*." Thus: "Action on behalf of justice and participation in the transformation of the world fully appear to us as a constitutive dimension of the preaching of the Gospel. . . ."[2]

My purpose is to reflect theologically on this language of the Synod, and on such notions as "social sin" and "sinful social structures." It seems to me that this language and the considerations which led to them are not only meaningful within the Christian tradition, but are also necessary for the life and health of the Church.

I will argue that the Christian notion of "forgiveness of sins"—hence of "sin"—is necessary to understand the full scope of the crisis our society is presently undergoing. These notions must be an essential part of the specifically Christian contribution to contemporary political life.

If this is so, then notions such as "social sin" are needed if Christianity is going to be relevant today, if Christianity is finally going to come to terms with the

Enlightenment and its consequence, our contemporary secular culture. And for this very reason, such notions are necessary if our faith is to be faithful to its originating Gospel source. For the Christian's faith needs always to be enmeshed with his daily life: if he believes that Jesus Christ is his Savior, he must have some idea of what it is he needs saving from. If he connects Christ's saving action only to his private sin, his private sorrow, then does this mean that his public concerns and the problems facing his nation and the world are aspects of his life which grace does not touch?

Let me put this another way before finishing these sketchy introductory remarks. The Gospel calls us to freedom. Christians have deeply understood what a full and terrible exercise of personal freedom the act of sinning is. Christians have also seen some of the *social consequences* of this exercise of freedom. I will be trying in this book to point out broader social consequences to individual acts of freedom than people normally take into account. But more important, I wish to raise the question of the *social pre-conditions* which are needed for individual acts of freedom, but which also restrict them.

Before I attack the problem of the meaningfulness of the phrase "social sin," I propose to examine the historical need for such a notion now. This will give us a historical framework within which to understand the notion, and will thereby give us most of the important elements needed to understand the notion.

Part I
Society's Need
for a Notion of Sin
and Forgiveness

Introduction

It is my conviction that Christians need not worry about the "relevance" of their faith in the contemporary world. The social world in which North Americans live is being shaken by crises. The Christian understanding of the mystery of sin and forgiveness is necessary, I contend, to grasp adequately the present crisis in our society.

In Part One I explore the need of contemporary society for a notion of social sin and forgiveness. Chapter 1 sketches the nature of the present crisis. Chapter 2 attempts to locate the historical roots of the crisis in the Enlightenment. I will argue that it was in overlooking the depth of the reality of sin and evil that our society invited the crisis it now faces. Chapter 3 tries to make this more specific by contrasting the modern scientific understanding of a social problem with a Christian sense of the mystery of evil and the need for pardon.

theologians, and that the task of these enlightened ones is to translate the message into terms understandable to the common man. I should, then, rephrase what was said about the role of theology. Perhaps it would be better to say that theology is a reflective attempt to ir-radiate contemporary man's attempt to grasp himself, his culture and his social order with the light of those symbols which cluster around the person of Jesus and his life, death and resurrection.

This might be a better starting point, since it si-tuates theology where today it ought to be, namely as part of that struggle to understand what it means to be human. Perhaps theology's role in this struggle could at one time remain implicit, but now it must be brought clearly to the fore. For our culture has become *his-torical-minded*. By this I mean that in the Atlantic community (Western Europe and North America) we have over the past two-hundred years more and more firmly come to see that our history is our responsibility. We feel called to create our story, which tells who we are. This story is all we have. It is our only answer to the question, what does it mean to be human?

Thus, there can be, at least in our time, no theolo-gy without an honest struggle to understand "the signs of the times." The theologian, like the historian, can put no meaningful question to his data from the past unless he is involved in his own generation's struggle for understanding and identity. But this is not all. Having been deeply influenced by the concerns of his time, the theologian can then bring to bear on these concerns the critical light which he derives from his tradition. It will be part of his duty to insist in every age that the most important single factor in the story of humanity is that one of us was God's own son, who died and rose again for our salvation. The human story is never simply the story of man's efforts. It must include the story of God's saving love for men. But this part of the story must be retold to fit with the rest. The theologian must understand how men are forging their story in his time so that he can speak meaningfully of man's slavery and of God's liberating saving grace now.

History and Illusion

It is important that the theologian understand the issues of his day, so that he can help people find out who they are and if and why they need saving. This task is important not simply so that men can be convinced of the truth of the Gospel. It is also needed in order that history progress toward humanization. For while it is true that as men face new historical challenges their understanding of the fullness of humanity grows, so it is also true that if their vision of humanity is narrowly comfortable, then they will not face challenges. The decline of civilizations, according to some great historians, occurs when communities coast on their achievements. They decide that the tried and true ways, which solved the problems of earlier times and made them great, will handle present problems as well. Newly emerging problems are not identified, not faced, not solved. They accumulate, merge; each complicates the other. Eventually the situation becomes unmanageable, unintelligible—even absurd because so much irrationality has gone into it. Decline sets in. Prophets point to the willful blindness, to the abuses; but no one can now devise solutions. Eventually collapse occurs.[1]

From this point of view, then, it is of enormous

ethical import that men's vision of humanity be as rich and broad and realistic as possible. Historical progress toward human happiness—and toward the realization of the Kingdom—is made not only by facing historical challenges but even more so by shattering the illusions to which men are prone. It seems that each time a community makes a breakthrough, it is tempted to idolize its latest achievement. It can do this only by overlooking some facet of humanity. Only by narrowing its view of man can the community claim that its laws and institutions serve man fully.

In times when people are smug and comfortable, the task of the theologian is to call for a fuller vision of humanity. But there are other times when the illusions, so carefully built up over generations, are brutally smashed by events. The twentieth century has, it seems, been such a time for Europeans and North Americans.

The bitter stripping began in Europe when the romantic belief in progress died in the mud of Flanders and on the hillside of Verdun. The first great socialist experiment degenerated into Stalinist terror. Finally, the traditional vindictive diplomacy which dictated the Treaty of Versailles combined with nationalism and economic collapse to lead Europe into the paroxysm of Nazi barbarism and yet another total war.

North Americans had to wait another generation. The agonies of Europe only served to confirm Americans in their belief that their peace and prosperity were merited because they were above traditional nationalist rivalries. And the paranoia of the Stalinist regime reinforced Americans' conviction that there was a direct connection between their political system in which they enjoyed civil liberty and the free-enterprise economic system.

Present Disillusion

Now, however, the United States strikes the sympathetic observer as a nation deeply wounded—the more deeply wounded because of its high ideals. America has seemed to so many for so long to be that one nation which had, through ingenuity, hard work and good fortune, solved the basic political and economic problems. It seemed to have merited the peace and prosperity which it enjoyed. Now it is called "Amerika" by many of its best young people.

The first uneasiness came with the protest movement of the blacks. During the early '60's, only the crudest racist could have objected. They demanded their civil rights; they affirmed the basic order of things; they only insisted that the nation live up to its own stated ideal. But suddenly, about 1968, the movement turned another direction. No longer was the goal amalgamation into a social order long since established by whites. Blackness was insisted upon: an irreducible, unassimilable culture. To understand this demand for a distinctive identity and not to construe it as separatism or treason is to acknowledge how high-handedly mainstream America has insisted on acceptance of its basic values as though the fullness of humanity could only be achieved through them. To understand the rage with which the blacks insist upon their distinctiveness is to see that

. . . the oppression of the black is so deeply woven into the institutions of America and hence into the consciousness of its people that it is almost impossible for the ordinary good person of common sense to discover it . . . . The situation of the negro can only be discovered by the person who is ready to *invert the categories* in which he has understood his national existence.[2]

What are some of these categories with which men understand their national existence? They are assumptions and perceptions, shared by practically everyone, which are so basic that they shape the social world which a group inhabits. For example, whites have for centuries inhabited a world where blacks have been inferior. White—at least, most middle class white—*assumptions* have included the superiority of abstract, theoretical thinking, of industrialization and resultant affluence, of democracy and civil tolerance; of rational, functional bureaucratic management; and finally of the repression and discipline required to live in a society holding such values. Given these values, and given the history of slavery in America and tribal culture in Africa the whites' *perceptions* of blacks are inevitable: they are good but simple folk, shiftless, irresponsible, incapable of making good citizens. Once, however, the affirmation that black is beautiful is made convincingly (even if only to blacks) this involves an inversion of white categories: what was once assuredly progress becomes madness or retrogression or, at best, one particular and rather narrow way to organize society.

Such an "inversion of categories" is what this book is about. I shall be trying in many ways to make clear the nature and need of such inversions, or transformations.

Besides the profound disillusion brought on by black protest, there was an even more savage ripping of the national fabric by the Vietnam war. Which made a deeper impact: stories of wanton savagery such as My

Lai and the bombing of cities, or the simple fact that America with all its technical might could not bend the will of the Vietnamese? Perhaps both these aspects of that war, its savagery and its futility, converge to highlight the same lesson: that affluence and know-how, so highly prized in America, lend neither right nor might in the face of human resistance. Think back to McNamara, a gentle urbane humanist, at his blackboard during press conferences, demonstrating with his statistics that he was getting a bigger bang for the buck and winning with his search and destroy missions. In early 1968 the Tet offensive showed that efficiency had not been effective. Did it take the stubbornness of this sad Vietnamese people, so long deprived of national sovereignty, so long divided by the presence of powerful outsiders, to teach us the impotence of technical efficiency in the face of human problems?

There is a third crisis slowly emerging. It again entails the "inversion of the categories" with which affluent North America has understood itself. This crisis concerns the relationship between the affluent and the poor in the world. In the last chapter I will discuss this crisis at length: but it must be mentioned early, since it hangs like a cloud over everything else I say.

When the Atlantic community learned to industrialize, it grew affluent and left the rest of the world in poverty. With the setting up of the United Nations, America and Europe embarked upon a program to "develop" the "underdeveloped" nations. In the mid-'60's, just as the blacks in the United States began to reject civil rights (and the implied assimilation), so there began a movement, especially in Latin America, to reject "development" as the goal of the non-industrialized nations and to aim for "liberation." Those who insist on "liberation" reject the implication in the word "development" that the poorer nations are less developed in a broad human sense and that they should develop according to the paradigms set by industrialized nations. "Liberation" points to the use of power by the rich, to the economic imperialism which keeps poorer nations underdeveloped.[3] They speak therefore of liberation.

The growth of this "liberation" movement in the Third World cannot but continue. Sometimes it will be the thinking behind armed revolution, sometimes it will inspire tough economic moves like those of the Allende government in Chile. Whatever the peoples of the Third World choose to do to back their demand for liberation, it will cause a crisis of conscience in the industrialized world. This crisis will absorb the first two crises I mentioned, for the illusion that modernization and its accompanying wealth has led to a fuller, happier humanity involves the illusions buried in the other two crises: the illusion that the white race is somehow superior to other peoples; the illusion that industrialization and wealth are "proofs" of this racial superiority; the illusion that growing aggregate wealth can make up for widening inequalities in the distribution of that increased wealth.

The time of choice in the face of this crisis seems near. The affluent world, with America in the lead, can continue to back economic mastery with military intervention. Even though some will be unsuccessful as in Vietnam, there are after all, the successes as well, such as the Dominican Republic. For every Algerian failure there is bound to be a Malaya success.

But it is also within the realm of possibility that the affluent peoples will recognize that the world which they have been putting together with such "success," the story which they have been telling, must be re-done. It is possible that the First World will examine its historical roots, the assumptions and decisions which have constituted its story since the modern era began and decide that there is a need to change those roots. Is there any part of the Christian message which the theologian can bring to bear to help bring about this "inversion of categories"? Is there any way to help Western man face disillusion without losing the will to rebuild?[4]

2
Roots of the Crisis

Western industrialized society is extraordinarily complex; not only is it complex, it boasts of being pluralistic, of providing people with many core visions around which the meaning of their life can cluster. Which elements of our contemporary culture seem most in need of transformation? Which basic categories with which people understand their existence seem most in need of inversion?

It strikes me as helpful to begin with two statements. First, our present society is, with all its complexity and pluralism, the heir both of the scientific method which was forged in the seventeenth century and of the vision of the eighteenth century Enlightenment which sought to remake our political understanding of ourselves on the basis of the new-found scientific method. Second, there has been from the beginning a profound tension between Christianity and the Enlightenment, between the forces of the intelligence and of faith, the great historical forces of the sacred and of the secular.

In this chapter I propose to explore the tension between Christianity and the Enlightenment. There has

not yet been a reconciliation. Any reconciliation must
be critical; Christians must learn to understand and
evaluate this modern world not necessarily on its own
terms, but in the light of the Christian tradition. But on
the other hand, the evaluation must be deeply respect-
ful; Christians cannot remain truculent outsiders.[1]
Christians must attain a sympathetic understanding of
the achievements of the secular project; only then will
we be able to offer a criticism which will contribute to a
creative, humanizing transformation of contemporary
culture. Conversely, this will be possible only if we
Christians learn to understand and cherish our own
tradition in the light of the achievements of the modern
world.

It might strike the astute reader (and I am sure
that you are astute) that I seem to be wandering all
over the field, tilting at any and every windmill when I
bring up the tension between Christianity and the Enlightenment. But it is right in line with the theme of this
little book. In the eighteenth century, the issue between
the philosophes[2] and the churchmen was basically concerned with the doctrine of the universal sinfulness of
man, and the moral ability of men to achieve a human-
ized, just society.

In affirming man's innocence, the philosophes
were not simply being shallow optimists. They had
caught a vision—an ethical vision—of man's autonomy
and his correlative responsibility for the shape of history. They were bent on underlining man's adulthood, his
dignity, his rationality; and they based their assertion
on the success of the scientific method. On the other
hand, the churchmen were not simply motivated by political conservatism. They were reasserting the fundamental mystery of the Christian faith, that Christ

had died and risen to save us from sin. They stood on the grounds of a biblical vision of sin as an all-or-nothing decision, involving even more than history—the eternal destiny of an individual person.

The Enlightenment sought innocence; Christianity began with belief in God's promise of pardon. They constitute two different visions of human freedom and of evil.

The Ethical Vision of the Enlightenment

It seems to me that the most important contribution of the Enlightenment to contemporary culture is the "ethical vision of the world" which it fashioned.

What do we mean here by an ethical vision of the world? If we take the problem of evil as the touchstone of the definition, we may understand by the ethical vision of the world *our continued effort to understand freedom and evil by each other.*[3]

Grandeur and courage were required to adopt this ethical vision: it is to insist that man and man alone is responsible for the evils of society and of history. It is to insist on man's moral autonomy, on his responsible adulthood. We are all heirs to this vision; upon it is based our historical-mindedness.

The Christian can at first only be perplexed by this aspect of the Enlightenment. He cannot but be moved by the moral grandeur of its ethical vision; and yet he cannot but be pained since this very ethical vision meant to the men of the time a rejection of Christianity. Indeed, this rejection becomes rage with some, such as Voltaire. Why could there not be an easy reconciliation? I turn here to Ernst Cassirer and to Peter Gay, historian of philosophy and historian, to try to piece together an answer.

Gay makes it clear that it is the Christian doctrine of original sin, of man's universal sinfulness and hence of his moral impotence, that so scandalizes and enrages the philosophes. For even if the Christian affirms man's dignity because he is God's son,

> . . . the point of Christian anthropology was that man is a son, dependent on God. Whatever the philosophes thought of man—innately decent or innately power-hungry, easy or hard to educate to virtue—the point of the Enlightenment anthropology was that man is an adult, dependent on himself.[4]

Cassirer has often stressed that there was no possible compromise between the Christians and the philosophes on this point. For the men of the Enlightenment were not simply trying to be shallow and overlook aspects of experience to which the Christian was pointing. They had glimpsed a new vision. Cassirer seems to have discovered this through his deep study of Kant: for Kant, austere and disciplined, had but one ornament in his study, a picture of Rousseau. What bond could there be between the measured man of reason and the tempestuous, brooding thinker whom the Romantics all claim as their father? Kant proclaimed Rousseau to be the Newton of the moral world.[5] Rousseau is perhaps the first man to think absolutely in ethical terms, in such wise that the religious dimension of human reality is denied. Rousseau wrestles with his own unshakeable

melancholy and with the evident evil in the world. After
the earthquake of Lisbon in 1755, men like Voltaire
were thrown from their earlier optimistic doctrine that
we live in the best of all possible worlds, but Rousseau
"the brooding and melancholy hermit" maintained a
"heroic optimism."[6] It is not an easy optimism, based
on wishful thinking. It is an optimism leading to an
ethical vision of unprecedented grandeur.

> Rousseau's one great principle—that man is good,
> that society makes him bad, but that *only* society,
> the agent of perdition, can be the agent of salva-
> tion . . . affirms not only that reform is desirable,
> but more important, that it is possible.[7]

It is out of the doctrine that man must and man
can reform society in order to reform himself that a
new ethical vision of society—and a new sense of responsibility for history—springs.

> But it is futile to hope that this salvation will be
> accomplished with outside help. No God can grant
> it to us; man must become his own savior and, in
> an ethical sense, his own creator. In its present
> form society has inflicted the deepest wounds on
> humanity; but society alone can and should heal
> these wounds. The burden of responsibility rests
> upon it from now on. . . . All contemporary social
> struggles are still moved and driven by this original
> stimulus. They are rooted in that consciousness of
> the *responsibility* of society which Rousseau was
> the first to possess and which he implanted in all
> posterity.[8]

It is doubtless true that much of the churchmen's criticism against this position was motivated by political conservatism. But they also had a counter-vision to uphold, a vision which began with belief in God's promise of pardon. For the ethical vision is both courageous and limited; it accepts responsibility for evil in history; but it will entertain consideration *only* of that evil which it can remedy. Perhaps it is better to understand the Enlightenment's proclamation of man's innocence as the undertaking to *search for innocence*: innocence is the goal rather than the beginning.[9] Since there is nobody to forgive him, man must make himself innocent once again through reform. But this means that man can only admit responsibility for those evils which are remediable through reform. He cannot entertain the full malice and destructiveness of sin, as does the Christian.

Thus it is that the vision of evil in modern society became tame and pallid. Unfortunately, there are practical results of taking so shallow a view of evil: a community is left without the analytic tools to grapple with the full reality of its problems. This seems to me to be operative in the debate between left and right in America today.

"Right" and "left" are of course, vague terms. It seems to me, however, that it is possible to identify a significant segment of the population today who would be considered politically conservative and yet who do not share the political vision of the classical conservative—the vision, say, of Edmund Burke. They seem much more to be the inheritors of a vision of innocence from the Enlightenment, the heirs of classical liberalism. Basically, they see only technical problems in public life. They see nothing problematic in the euphoric prediction that if we could put a man on the moon, we surely can solve the problems of our cities. More concretely, people of this opinion are convinced that our technical ability to maintain a sufficient level of economic growth will in the end solve all other social problems.

Those on the "left" are also a disparate group. One common characteristic, especially among the young, is that they speak very much in terms of good and evil. They have all heard in freshman English courses that one dominant theme in American literature identifies the American, especially the frontiersman, with the New Adam in search of a new innocence. They are shocked that America's self-perception of being innocent has led to extremely aggressive behavior. For they have heard, too, that violence is as American as cherry pie.

But their distance from the mainstream liberal view is not complete; their criticism does not probe to the roots of our culture. For while the liberal-conservatives insist on America's innocence, the young seek a lost innocence and seek it innocently. In a thoughtful passage, Rollo May remarks:

Innocence as a virtue has gone rancid . . . capitalizing on naiveté, it dwells in a childhood never outgrown. It . . . cannot come to terms with the destructiveness in one's self or others . . . and hence . . . becomes self-destructive.[10]

He reflects on the symbolism of Allison Krause dropping flowers in the barrel of a Guardsman's rifle, only to be killed by a stray (whatever that might mean) bullet from one of those same rifles the next day. Can

innocence insist on remaining innocent, guileless, obli-
vious of destructive tendencies and decisions in others—
and still remain innocent? Dr. May insists that innocence must grapple with evil, come to terms with it,
absorb it. I am insisting that this is only possible if the
evil is *forgiven*. I find that the necessity of forgiveness is
an essential element of the biblical ethical vision.

The Ethical Vision of the Bible

The ethical vision of the world is set forth at the
very beginning of the Bible. The Jahwist account of the
beginnings of the human race make it clear: evil entered
history through the sin of Adam (Gen. 3).

Further, the Bible understands sin in the deepest
and most far-reaching terms. To sin is not simply to
undergo ritual defilement; it is not simply to break
rules; it is not simply to fail to achieve full growth.

The prophet Hosea is the first to break through to
a deeply personal notion of sin. His life is a lived parable. He took a wanton for a wife. "Go, marry a whore,
and get children with a whore, for the country itself has
become nothing but a whore by abandoning Yahweh"
(Hos. 1, 2). She forsakes him to become a prostitute in
the temple of Baal. Hosea forgives her.

> Yahweh said to me, "Go a second time, give your
> love to a woman, loved by her husband but an
> adulteress in spite of it, just as Yahweh gives his
> love to the sons of Israel" (Hos. 3, 1).

Two themes are clear here. First, any deep, theological consideration of sin is under the sign of forgive-

ness. In fact, it is the forgiveness of sin which is central
to the biblical and Christian tradition; the notion of sin
unfolds as the mystery of forgiveness is probed. Sec-
ondly, from Hosea we learn first that sin is a personal
affront to the living, loving God. It is infidelity to the
covenant to which God is always faithful.

Sin, then, is a separation from God. But this
means that to sin is to consign oneself to nothingness.
The Old Testament has many passages elaborating the
destructive emptiness of sin. Perhaps the conclusion to
solemn discourse of Moses on giving the Israelites the
Law says it best:

I set before you life or death, blessing or curse.
Choose life, then, so that you and your descen-
dents may live, in the love of Yahweh your God,
obeying his voice, clinging to him; for in this your
life consists (Dt. 30, 15. 19-20).

Because the choice means so much, it becomes
part of the prophetic notion of sin that this choice is
inescapably personal:

Why do you keep repeating this proverb in the
land of Israel:

"The fathers have eaten unripe grapes;
and the children's teeth are set on edge?"

As I live—it is the Lord Yahweh who speaks—
there will no longer be any reason to repeat this
proverb in Israel. See now: all life belongs to me;
the father's life and the son's life, both alike belong
to me. The man who has sinned, he is the one who
shall die (Ez. 18, 2-4).

These themes are picked up and deepened in the New Testament. In the Synoptics and the writings of St. John, the central message is that Jesus saves from sin. The notion of sin is developed only to highlight the full implications of Jesus' saving act.

Jesus' basic message, the Good News, is, according to Mark (1, 5) and Matthew (4, 17), "repent." Jesus' mission—indeed his very name—is "he is the one who is to save his people from their sins" (Mt. 1, 21). "Jesus" means "Jahweh saves."

Sin is separation from God. In the parable of the Prodigal Son, Luke understands sin to be going away from the Father's house (Lk. 15, 11-32). John, in his gospel uses other metaphors to underscore sin as separation from God: to be in sin is to be in darkness (Jn. 3, 19-21), it is to be without life (Jn. 4, 35-36).

> "Neither Jesus nor the primitive community asked concerning the nature of sin; they saw men in the reality of sins which were very definitely individual sins. The work of Christ is based on this reality . . . it was the theologian Paul who raised the theological question of sin as a power which determines the nature of man and world, and who saw its actuality as such." [11]

It is especially in his letter to the Romans that Paul elaborates his vision of the cosmic, historic, eschatological implications of Christ's saving us from sin. The unhappiness of his contemporaries he ascribes not simply to limitation or blindness, but to sin (Chapter 1). He is clear about the origin of sin in the world: it is through one man (Chapter 5). Not only sin, but death (sin's wages) and all other evils have plagued men be-

cause of one man. To be in sin is to be unrighteous, es-
tranged from God. It is also to be under the yoke of the
devil (Chapter 7).

Paul subscribes to the ethical vision. Not only is
the goodness or badness of each man dependent upon
his free choice, but the lot of all history has been and is
dependent upon human freedom.

But if Paul is the first man in the history of human
literature to face the full import of the universality of
human sinfulness, if he is the first to say clearly that all
evil entered history through the sin of man, if he is the
first to say clearly that all men everywhere have been
affected in their very being by that sin—he says all this
only to bring out the depth of his belief in the saving
power of "one man." The structure of Chapter 5 of his
Letter to the Romans makes this clear; it builds to the
climax that grace superabounds.

This "Christological vision" of the world clearly
takes away from the absoluteness of the Enlightenment's ethical vision. It begins not with human freedom, but with God's forgiving love. It begins there not
to derogate from human freedom, but only to assert, in
the face of sin, with the more fullness and force, the
mystery of human freedom.

Summary

In this first Part, I am trying to develop an understanding of the need for the Christian sense of sin and
hope for pardon in order to grasp the full extent of the
crisis facing our society. Forces are gathering which
challenge the assumptions of Western, industrialized
nations: assumptions concerning the racial and cultural

superiority of the whites; assumptions concerning war; assumptions concerning the humanizing effect of technology and affluence. The rich and powerful nations can muster their strength in an effort to crush these challenges. On the other hand, they can read in the challenges a call to become transformed, to strip away historical illusions in order to become more fully human and free.

In this chapter I have begun to probe a fundamental illusion of the Western world, namely that as inheritors of the ethical vision of the Enlightenment we have accepted a resolutely broad responsibility for the shaping of our historical destiny: but in so doing we have adopted a superficial, partial vision of evil. I have outlined the far deeper biblical vision of human sin, and insisted that this deeper vision is possible only to the person who believes that forgiveness is available.

This contrast between the Enlightenment ethical vision and the Christological vision of the Bible now must be explored. We need some inkling of the reasons for each of these positions. I propose to examine these reasons in the next chapter.

3
Science and the Mystery of Evil

When the philosophes proclaimed mankind's moral autonomy and ability to shape history, they also insisted on mankind's innocence. Were the philosophes simply overlooking an important segment of human experience—the experience of human limitation and perversity—when they declared mankind innocent?

The basis of their insistence on human innocence was the breathtaking new experience of the success of the scientific method. How important was the forging of the scientific method? No less a historian than Herbert Butterfield says that the breakthrough of modern science in the seventeenth century

. . . outshines everything since the rise of Christianity and reduces the Renaissance and Reformation to the rank of mere episodes, mere internal displacements, within the system of medieval Christendom.[1]

Since the scientific way of looking at things is so important in our contemporary culture, I wish to explore the connection between it and the ethical vision of the Enlightenment as described in the last chapter. I will try to show that science as a way of looking at things assumes that reality is *commensurable* with the human mind. That is, the scientific vision assumes that all things can be thoroughly, adequately understood. There is no room for mystery in the scientific world. It was this assumption of commensurability which enabled the philosophes to declare the moral autonomy of mankind and accept the ethical vision.

I will contrast this experience of the Enlightenment with the religious experience of *disproportion* which leads the Christian to affirm with sorrow the mystery of evil. As I pointed out in the last chapter, nobody can face the mystery of evil without first being assured of the possibility of forgiveness. In this chapter, I will also explore the mystery of forgiveness as a requisite to the full understanding of the contemporary social crisis.

Science and the Autonomy of the Human Reason

It is important, I think, to see why the philosophes spoke of the great scientific figures of the seventeenth century, men like Galileo and Newton, as the liberators of mankind.

Perhaps the most obvious way in which science liberated men was that it brought security. Earlier visions of the world had given men a sense of order, but it was a mysterious order, in which they could only stand in fearful awe. The majestic sweep of Newton's vision might well have inspired awe, but men were liberated from fear. Newton was praised all over Europe and America because he had set men free and put them in control of nature. He had unlocked her secrets.[2]

Science brought security because it worked. It was a method which enabled men to break problems down into simple, practical, answerable questions. For instance, when Galileo was working out his theory of mechanics, he did not ask the questions the medievals had asked. They had wondered what kept a cannon ball in the air: was it the angels? was it an inherent quality called impetus? He asked another kind of question: where will the cannon ball land? His question can be answered quite precisely. His sort of question leads to the ability to predict. It works; it gives men control.

Science provided men not only with a method which worked in the age-old struggle with a niggardly nature, but also with an escape from the scandal of oppression and division. Precisely because it worked, precisely because it asked simple questions to which there were palpably correct (or incorrect) answers, it was a method which vindicated man's dignity, his rationality, his autonomy.

Christianity, on the other hand, spoke of murky mysteries which nobody could understand. Assent was, therefore, commanded by external authority—ecclesiastical authority—based, so claimed the philosophes, on superstition and fear. Science for its part appealed only to men's intelligence; it laid its claim to men's consent only its own internal rationality and argument. *Science seeks only to convince, never to compel.* To affirm scientific findings was to be free, not to be oppressed.

Because all men were capable of verifying the claims of science, they would also be rid of division. The Hundred Years War was still vivid to men in the late seventeenth century and early eighteenth century.

Christianity, even with its message of love, had divided
men and provided them with such epithets as "sinner"
and "heretic," thereby legitimatizing wars and persecu-
tions. Here was a new knowledge which united. Best of
all, it united not by suppressing all divisions and hesi-
tancies, but it united by convincing all.[3]

There is a popular notion to explain why science is
able to convince so thoroughly. It is because—so goes
this popular explanation—science is objective. It simply
lays before people the facts. It is a method based on ob-
servation. It does not build intellectual houses of cards;
it is much more humble; it simply tells us what is.

This view of scientific objectivity claims that a scientific model is a mirror image of reality. It assumes
that external reality is already structured into constella-
tions of facts. Scientists discover these facts, and set
them forth in convenient resumes, called models.

Science, however, is more complex. The scientific
method is not simply a matter of taking facts into account. It constitutes, in Butterfield's words, a "different
kind of thinking-cap, a transposition in the mind of the
scientist himself. . . ."[4] This new thinking-cap consists
in concentrating only on those aspects of reality to
which numbers can be assigned. Whenever science asks
a question it wants an exhaustive answer, open to verifi-
cation by any competent observer. In order to achieve
this utter clarity and exhaustive verifiability, it leaves
out any aspect of reality which is fuzzy or murky or
mysterious.[5]

There is no doubt that the abstractions effected by
the scientific method have led to enormous gains for
mankind. But it should be recognized that the invention
of the scientific method was not simply a discovery of
empirical reality. It was a construction, based on a

choice: certain aspects of reality are dealt with very effectively at the cost of leaving other aspects of reality out of account altogether.

The Prosaic Mind:
The Commensurability of Mind and Reality

As we saw in Chapter 2, one of the key reasons why the Enlightenment philosophes saw the Christian tradition as their enemy was because of the doctrine of man's sinfulness. My reading of the matter is that they were right to see that to adopt the newly forged scientific method was to overlook the reality and mystery of evil. One of the costs involved in the modern decision to go for the gains of the scientific method is that the reality of evil gets overlooked. A preoccupation with the religious questions of death and sin will bring no *pragmatic* gain. I fully agree: but perhaps part of the malaise experienced today finds its roots in the decision to become scientific. Evil remains a reality, but now we find ourselves in a culture which has lost the ability to come to terms with this reality—at least in public.

Many people have, over the years, criticized science for its limitation of vision. Doubtless, we have to distinguish between the enterprise of science and that mindset, derived from scientific successes, which in a more or less popular form helps to shape contemporary culture. There needs to be a distinction also between the mindset which people turn to in their everyday private life and that mindset which governs the questions entertained by governments and bureaucrats. Certainly the experience of three years' living in Canada's national capital has taught me that reality within a federal bureaucracy is distorted and does not reflect the reality lived across the country. In the capital the preoccupation with administrative problems and the inability of the tone-setters to grasp problems in any but economic terms gives the observer an exaggerated impression of how deeply the culture is affected by the scientific mindset.

George Morgan is a thoughtful observer of contemporary culture. He speaks of the "prosaic mind." He stresses that the prosaic mind is not coterminous with the scientific mind: few, he remarks, have the "reasoning power, the discipline, the respect for truth and the precision that science demands."[6] Nevertheless the characteristics of the prosaic mind which he spells out have a great affinity with the characteristics of science which we recounted above. The prosaic man, he says, is interested in "facts." Morgan reads this interest in facts to mean that the prosaic man's interest is in abstraction, the kind of abstraction to which numbers can be assigned. The prosaic man is also interested in procedures, techniques; he wants clear-cut boundaries, nothing fuzzy; he stresses literalness, wants everything spelled out explicitly; and regards objectivity as the essence of reliability and truthfulness. Science brings exhaustive light to a subject, spelling out all the factors with precision and utter explicitness: in this way it commands consent by its inner perspicuity. If it cannot bring this kind of light to a problem it leaves it alone, leaves it in darkness.[7] Similarly, the prosaic mind tends to reject as "meaningless" any question for which it cannot find a complete answer.

It seems to me that both the strength and weakness of the scientific method are summed up in the word *commensurability*. The revolutionary geniuses of the seventeenth century forged a new method of analyzing reality: they succeeded in bracketing the mystery and in learning to concentrate on those abstract characteristics with which the human mind was commensurate, that is, which it could understand exhaustively. But this achievement exacted its own cost: men had to leave out of account those aspects of reality which were not and never would be commensurate with the human mind.

The Experience of Evil: Disproportion

Pascal, who was one of the outstanding scientists of the seventeenth century, a mathematician, inventor of the calculating machine, was at the same time an intense if gloomy religious thinker. (Voltaire, who was obsessed by him, called him "that sublime misanthrope.") Pascal, in his famous *pensée* on disproportion says,

> Men have rashly undertaken to probe into nature as if there were some proportion between themselves and her.[8]

This is clearly a comment upon the enterprise of science itself. Here, at least, is one scientist who saw clearly the limitations of science.

In this fragment on disproportion, Pascal is developing what Ricoeur calls a "rhetoric of misery," an initial exploration of the feeling of dread: "The eternal silence of these infinite spaces fills me with dread."[9] Pascal moves from a spatial image—man is confronted by the infinity of outer space and the infinitesimal atomic particles—to the disproportion between men's mind and these disparate realities. Pascal leaves unspoken the connection between this disproportion and his misanthropic musings on man's corruption. Others, however, have taken up the thread.

First of all, is this a common experience, this disproportion? I would suggest that it is, though most people could not or would not think to put that name on their experience. It is the experience of being driven toward totality and yet of being "thrown" (Heidegger's word) up against tiny pieces: fragments of reality experienced within fragments of time by fragments of myself. I know that love should be a totalizing experience and I want it to be. But my love is torn: I must grope my way toward love, which will bring coherence to my life, through distractions of all sorts. We must learn to love despite (and through) our work, our children, money cares, other friends, political concerns. And finally, "if all goes well," the unity we achieve will be shattered by death. To me the most mysterious part of the marriage vow is that after working a lifetime at loving, each spouse undertakes the risk of burying the other.

We are confronted with the same disproportion in public life. The more aware I become of my responsibility to contribute to the coherence and development of man's story, history, the more sharply I am aware of how I can only contribute by working for a political party with whose entire platform and personnel I cannot agree. I must take sides on certain political or social issues, the parameters of which I know have been arrived at by compromise. And again, even if the people and programs I work for were exactly to my taste, so that my efforts were undiluted by compromise, still I must recognize that my motivation to work for the fullness of history can only be frustrated by my death. Even if the fragmentation of opinions is overcome, even if we could thread together the perfect program despite the refractoriness of each element—even then only posterity would benefit, for we cannot even imagine overcoming the fragmentation of history over time. And so the wisecrack "What has posterity done for me?" becomes, in the end, the great barrier to historical progress.

The disproportion can be understood in religious terms as well. I am made by God and for God. I can find fulfillment only in God. Yet I am cast into a world of shadow. All my attempts to know and love him directly through a life of prayer are subject to illusion and disappointment. In the end, I am cast back upon my neighbor: who can love God, whom he has never seen, if he does not love his brother, whom he can see? (Cf. 1 John, 5, 20). I must piece my love for God together, with the bits and pieces of reality, through the shards of time, which are my lot.

We encounter in these experiences not simply limitation or finiteness; we encounter the specific human limitation, which discloses itself as a rift, a tear, a fault in our deepest being.[10] This rift can be set forth in metaphysical terms: the disproportion and unending tension between spirit and matter. It can be set forth in religious terms: the unbridgeable gap between God, our last end, and creatures, in terms of which I must seek God. It can be set forth in anthropological terms: the fullness of my being is a task to be accomplished in the fullness of my future; but, as T.S. Eliot said, "my life is measured out in coffee spoons." I possess my future only through the commitments about this or that which

I make in this present moment. Totality, which is what my being strives for, can only be approached fragmentarily, asymptotically.

This rift in my being is the locus of the possibility of evil. It is in this irreduceable tension that I experience my terrible "ability"—which is and is not simply an "inability"—to do evil. The connection between the fragments of which my life consists and the totality toward which I tend is not clear to see nor easy to accomplish. The medievals saw the root of moral evil in *acedia*, a deep lassitude which whispers that it is not worth the effort. The temptation is to give up hope, to cease to try to put the future together by putting myself together now. Short-term goals come to define my horizon; selfish considerations predominate. Each fragment of reality which I encounter has a goodness of its own: it is pleasurable; it is useful; it contributes to the coherence of my life as I have decided, according to my narrow vision, to put it together. Let the rest go. How can I bother with long-term goals, with overall considerations, with the coherence of history, with the aspirations of freedom fighters in southern Africa, with the dying in Calcutta?

And thus human evil emerges. For this is not a simple choice among competing options. This is a decision against being human in its fullness. This is a decision to shut out of my life part of my reality. It is a decision to keep my horizon narrow. Seen in a religious perspective it is, in Thomas Aquinas' words, a turning away from God and toward creatures.

The Mystery of Forgiveness

The Christian is not being perverse in affirming the

mystery of evil. It is experience which leads to this affirmation. However, it is not an affirmation which men make gladly. The human mind shies away from the destructiveness of evil and would rather overlook it.

It is clear, as I insisted in Chapter 2, that the biblical tradition does not dwell upon evil for its own sake, but only to bring out the saving, forgiving power of God's love. The Christian tradition proclaims the forgiveness of sin in its creeds, not the persistence of sin.

How is the mystery of forgiveness to be understood within the perspective which I have been trying to develop in this book? I wish to develop briefly the nature and the need of forgiveness from the standpoint of both human ethical growth and Christian theological tradition.

The perspective which I developed in the last section sees the primary ethical task to be fidelity: one becomes a person by freely accepting responsibility for an emerging pattern of meaning in one's life. A person is one who stands by his story, who has attained the integrity (i.e. wholeness) whereby his actions and words reflect who he is and what his life stands for. To be a person is, in other words, to be faithful to one's word. For what else have we but gestures and words, strung together over time, with which to weave our story?

Each person, then, must exercise responsible freedom to decide and, over time, to effect who he is going to be. Authentic depth is achieved only if there is continuity and coherence knitting the several decisions into one biography. Because decisions, if they are person-building, shape a person's future, pull it together, give it thrust and purpose, these decisions are better called commitments.

The philosophical problem of infidelity then becomes clear: infidelity to commitment means inauthenticity, fragmentation, incoherence. But how can someone whose story—whose very person—has become broken up and spasmodic and incoherent ever find the purpose to pull himself together?

Robert Bolt, in *A Man for All Seasons*, has said this as well as anyone. The play is about Thomas More. In the past few generations, More's reputation has improved greatly. In the late nineteenth century he was considered by most educated Englishmen to have been a puzzle. He was a witty, urbane humanist, one of the finest products of the new learning of the Renascence. Later he was a wise, humane and scrupulously honest judge. But in refusing to take the Oath of Supremacy, he seemed—according to earlier generations—to have simply reverted from the best of the new moderns to a narrow medieval. Latterly, however, his image has been enhanced. He is seen as an existentialist hero, a man who retains his authenticity in the face of social pressure, political disgrace and death. This is how Bolt sees him. Bolt has More's daughter Margaret counsel him to "say the words of the oath and in your heart think otherwise."

More replies:

When a man takes an oath, Meg, he's holding his own self in his own hands. Like water (cups hands) and if he opens his fingers *then*—he needn't hope to find himself again.[11]

Why is it that the inauthentic man—the unfaithful man—has not within himself the resources to become authentic? His decision to be inauthentic is not, as we have seen, neutral. He has opted against human growth. He has chosen a narrow base; he is attempting to build the meaning of his life with narrow limits. He refuses to look beyond those limits. Because the thirst for coherence is so strong and because considerations which take him past his self-imposed limits will upset the coherence of his life, he fast loses the moral ability to see beyond his limits.

He doubtless had plausible motives for his original inauthentic decision. Nobody ever makes a decision *because* it leads to inauthenticity. Nobody ever sins *because* it is sinful: everyone has speciously good reasons for what he does. Upon this destructively narrow original decision, a cramping but ever tougher coherence is maintained. Broader considerations, calculated to upset this narrower coherence, will have to come to him from another.

The question then remains, in what form must these new considerations come? Often they come in a threatening way. People are told to change or be punished. This tends, it seems, simply to reinforce the defensive patterns of the earlier inauthentic coherence.

Even if a person were, when reprimanded or threatened by another, to recognize the potential destructiveness of the patterns embodying his inauthentic decision, this does not mean that he will be able to change. For if his original decision was truly dehumanizing and destructive, then there will be no recognizable continuity between his present stance and the new stance being called for. He will see no way out. His reaction can only be self-revulsion and despair.

While there can be no continuity at the level of content (or thrust) between an inauthentic decision and the called-for authentic decision, there can still be con-

tinuity at a deeper, personal level. That is, if the call for
change includes not only condemnation of the earlier
pattern but also loving affirmation of the person
trapped in that pattern, then there emerges for that person the moral possibility of change.

There is, then, a possibility of a man finding himself again even after he has fragmented himself by infidelity and walled himself into patterns of specious and
narrow coherence. Another person can point him toward the possibility of a fuller self with an affirming yet
correcting word. Another can forgive him and open up
the hope of change.

The Christian tradition has always maintained that
Jesus' call to repentence contained both a condemnation of sin and an undying love for the sinner. The
biblical vision of sin as opting for nothingness over
against God, outlined in Chapter 2, is perhaps the full-
est expression of what I am trying to say. Once a man
has separated himself from God and has decided to
stand alone, relying on his own resources, what hope is
there of him finding life or of finding God again, unless
God forgives him and calls to him to return? There is a
scheme of images in the Bible which sees man separated from God as nothing, as vanity, as "less than a
breath of air" (Ps. 62, 9; Is. 40, 17).

Paul, reflecting on the mystery of man's sinfulness
and God's forgiving love, has developed for us in his
Letters to the Romans and the Galatians the doctrine
of "justification by faith." Left to himself, a man will
transgress the Law, for the Law brings out to man his
deep sinfulness. But even if a man did obey the Law, he
would not attain righteousness but only a hollow self-
righteousness. "No one can be justified in the sight of
God by keeping the Law: all that law does is to tell us

what is sinful" (Rom. 3, 20). "So what becomes of our boasts [for having kept the law]? There is no room for them" (Rom. 3, 27).

Justice, goodness, authenticity—that which constitutes full human personhood and is the inescapable responsibility of each person—is, in Paul's view, the gratuitous gift of a forgiving God to a sinner already dead in his sin (Rom. 8). This is the mystery of forgiveness proclaimed by Christians—a forgiveness which renders men free and makes possible full human dignity.

With his simile of spilled water, Robert Bolt has made clear the impossibility of the inauthentic man regaining integrity. In the face of this radical impossibility the Christian, grasping the significance of Christ's resurrection, affirms his hope in God's forgiveness.

Summary: The Need for the Christian Hope of Pardon in a Technological Culture

The Enlightenment proclaimed man's autonomy and man's responsibility. Our contemporary, historical-minded society is the heir to that proclamation. How much of a piece is any culture, especially a culture such as ours which so prides itself on being pluralistic? Does it make sense to say that our culture, in making the historic choice to become scientific and technical, in choosing in a throughgoing way for men's autonomy, has chosen to overlook the mystery of evil? I do not want to overstate my case.

On the one hand, there are many within our culture who are painfully aware of the reality of evil in the world. On the other hand, in the public domain there are clear indications that we have never opted to be consistently and always technical in our outlook or our decisions.

I would however suggest that there is a tendency in our culture to think that what has gone wrong is only a matter of limits—especially limits of knowledge, limits of policy—as essentially technical problems to be corrected. This, I would suggest, has happened because our success through science and technology has occurred precisely because we became practical, and bracketed (i.e., systematically overlooked) the rift in our being. This systematic oversight was made both possible and legitimate because it is clearly beyond the purview of science to entertain notions such as the love of God and the overall coherence of human history. Such notions are murky and mysterious. And it was only through a method whose prime goal was public verifiability coupled with exhaustive intelligibility that men would achieve the goal of unity with autonomy.

There is, then, an unspoken assumption behind the adoption of the scientific method as the core of our culture. This is that there is no ultimately refractory reality, that all things ultimately are capable of rational ordering, that all things will eventually cohere. This view leaves out of account malice, persistent bad faith and bad will. It leaves out of account the necessity and the possibility of conversion and of forgiveness.

Evil does not constitute a technical problem: it is not commensurate with the human mind; it is not exhaustively intelligible; it does not admit of gradual piecemeal solution. Evil is opaque; it is irrational, rooted in irrationality. It makes no sense to choose fragmentation, chaos and the eventual destruction of one's being over the coherence, integration and the eventual fullness of one's being. The choice between good and evil is not a simple alternative between things of the same order. It is the choice between all or nothing.

It seems unlikely if not impossible that anyone can bear to admit that he has chosen nothingness instead of the fullness of his humanity. Certainly such an admission would be a despairing one if forgiveness were not assured. I ended the first Chapter by asking if there was anything Christianity could contribute to help Western man face the disillusion which history is forcing upon him without his losing the will to rebuild.

The Christian belief in God's promise of forgiveness is necessary for contemporary technological culture if it is to face its present crises. The Christian should be devising ways to invite contemporary secular man to take his sinfulness fully into account in order to be truly free, that is, in order to be forgiven.

This is the *historic need*, as I see it, for the notion of "social sin" in our day. It is the correlative to forgiveness, a notion which our culture has lost the ability to entertain publicly. We need now to turn to the second part of our inquiry, namely what "social sin" or "sinful social structures" might mean.

Part II
The Notion of
Social Sin

Introduction

As I understand the matter, the secular culture which has felt itself heir to the Enlightenment has forged a courageous and sweeping ethical vision of men's responsibility for the shape of history and society. The men who adopted this broad vision found the courage to do so in the success of the scientific method. This meant that the breadth of their ethical vision entailed a shallowness with respect to their notion of evil. Because they assumed that all reality was commensurate to the human mind, they could at last proclaim the autonomy of human rationality; but they thereby overlooked the full depth of the opaque mystery of human evil, of human malice, of human perversity. They overlooked, in a word, the necessity of men being forgiven.

Thus it is my contention that, in its present crisis, modern Western culture needs to rediscover the sense of sin and of being forgiven which is central to the Christian tradition. But, on the other hand, the Christian community is in no position to convince the modern secular mainstream that it has anything serious to offer to the contemporary who is agonizing over the current crisis. Far from being a corrective prophetic presence in today's world, the Christian community tends only to reinforce the worst in modern culture by insisting on an individualist notion of sin.

4
Sinful Social Structures

The Christian Church has clung to a private, individualist notion of sin. What are the motives for this individualist tendency? It is unlikely that the majority of Christians are motivated by a conservative political position. Church leaders, it is true, often seem to have the same point of view as other big proprietors; and seem to exhibit the "prudence" required of the guardians of large holdings or of the administrators of large organizations, rather than the folly of the cross. But, just as I sought the best motives of the philosophes (without straining the reader's credulity) when they denied human sinfulness, so here I would like (with the same proviso) to look for the Christian's best motives.

What is key is the connection between, on the one hand, the Christian's theological vision of the all-or-nothing stakes of the individual drama of sin and salvation, and on the other hand, the Christian's insistence that "full knowledge and full responsibility" are characteristic of sin. In the Christian view, each person is called forth into existence by a loving God; God calls each of us by name to an unending life of love with him. But the mystery of human freedom is such that

each person must accept or reject this call. Everything
hangs on that decision. This "eschatological" vision of
sin does not take kindly to loose talk that a shopper in
a supermarket in Peoria who buys a pound of coffee is
"responsible" for Portuguese oppression of Angolan
coffee workers. Too much is at stake to admit this kind
of responsibility.

Within the Catholic community this individualistic
notion of sin seems to have another more practical
root. Catholic theology of sin has until very recently
been worked out by men who were also confessors—
and worked out for confessors. The starting point has
been an equation between "it is a sin" and "it must be
confessed." This has led to an almost exclusive concern
with private guilt: with those actions for which a person
had full knowledge and for which he must accept full
responsibility.

The Christian, in order to convince his secular contemporary that the Good News of forgiveness is necessary today, must keep the depth of his traditional vision, but broaden his notion of responsibility so that it
encompasses not merely private sin, but also the great
political issues of the day. I am not advocating that the
Christian fudge his notion of responsibility. I do not
hold any notion of collective guilt, which would weaken
the traditional Christian tenet that responsibility is inescapably personal. I am arguing that one of the modern
Christian's chief responsibilities is to extend the limits
of his conscious responsibility. If the Christian faith is
to be an active, saving force in today's historical world,
then Christians must undertake to have "full knowledge" and take "full responsibility" for more than their
own private lives. Let us explore this further in this
chapter.

Biblical Testimony about the Power of Sin

As we saw in the previous chapter, biblical tradition affirms the ethical vision unequivocally. But if the ethical vision concentrates on the evil that men do, the Scriptures speak also of the evil which men suffer.

The Jahwist account of the Adam story (Gen. 3) makes it clear that evil entered the world through the agency of human freedom. Yet at that very moment, the Jahwist dramatizes, in the figure of the snake and in the conversation between Adam and Eve, the experience of *being tempted.*

While sin can be recognized to be vanity, emptiness, the nothingness of being away from God, yet each serious person experiences sin as power, as a threatening force which is at the same time beguiling. While each person must recognize that he has allowed himself to be seduced, yet it is also true that he has been seduced. A person who stands in the biblical tradition will have to accept personal responsibility for guilt; yet his own experience as well as countless biblical passages will point him to all for which he is not responsible, but which weighs in on him enticing him, frightening him, almost forcing him to sin.[1]

Paul, in his Letter to the Romans, has, as we have seen, worked out fully the ethical vision in the light of the risen Christ. But Paul speaks also of the power of sin.

In my inmost self I dearly love God's law, but I can see that my body follows a different law that battles against the law which my reason dictates. This is what makes me a prisoner of that *law of sin* which lives inside my body (Rom. 7, 22-23).

Paul is not here speaking of some material principle which is evil. He is talking of a law of sin. Throughout his Letter to the Romans he speaks of the power
which sin has over us. He speaks of the "reign of sin"
and the reign of death (the latter being the sign of the
former). Men can be "slaves of sin that leads to death";
Christ has saved us from this "slavery of sin." (Rom. 6,
15-19) In this usage, "sin" seems to be other than a free
human choice: it is a universal condition, a power external to man and over man.

It is, I believe, in the interplay between these two
experiences of sin, namely, the reign of sin and the sinful act, that we will find meaning for the notion "social
sin" or "sinful social structure."

I find that John's use of the word "world" is perhaps the best to help us in our reflections. There are
three poles to his complex thought. First, to speak of
the world is not to speak of some principle of evil, as
though God were responsible for the good, and some
other force, the world, were responsible for evil. For the
world has its being through the Word: it is created by
God (Jn. 1, 10). Indeed, "God loved the world so much
that he gave his only Son" (Jn. 3, 16).

On the other hand, the world has been judged (Jn.
12, 31) for the "whole world lies in the power of the
Evil One" (1 Jn. 5, 19).

Nothing the world has to offer,
   the sensual body,
   the lustful eye,
   pride in possessions,
could ever come from the Father
but only from the world (1 Jn. 2, 16).

John speaks of the light of Christ overcoming the darkness of the world. The contrast is complete.

The third pole in John's thought is that men are before a choice. Disciples of Jesus are not to belong to this world (Jn. 15, 19). They are not to love the world (1 Jn. 2, 15).

This language about "world" is a dramatic way to talk about the dynamics of sin which we all experience. For this world of which John speaks is not something apart from men. It is the place where men live; more exactly, it is the result of *men's interaction*. The story of the fall includes not only the figure of the snake to symbolize the mysterious ways in which man is lured to sin. Perhaps more to our purpose, the story also includes the interplay between the man and the woman. The Jahwist rejects this interplay as an exoneration. But he clearly means to encapsule everyone's experience. Man could not be alone. He needed community. Yet one of the key factors in his sinful decision was his being in community.

The ethical vision focuses on one aspect of sin, namely, on *guilt*, on the terrible consequences of the individual act of sinful freedom. It brings out the fragmentation of guilt: it singles out the isolation, the loneliness of the guilty conscience which cannot shift the blame; it beams a narrow, intense light on the disruptive power of the sinful act to destroy the coherence, the meaning of a person's life.

But the Scriptures also speak of the universality and the power of sin. When Paul insists that all men sin he is not reporting on a statistical headcount. He means that all men share a *solidarity*, a *complicity in sin*.[2]

I sometimes have the impression that theologians shy away from dwelling on this overwhelming experi-

ence people have of complicity in sin.[3] It seems that
theologians are afraid that such talk would lead people
to feel excused, or that it might offend against the doctrine of human freedom. Yet every parent who tries to
monitor what his or her children see on television, every
parent who is wheedled by children to buy in order to
keep up with neighbors' children knows perfectly well
how the community in which we live exerts enormous
pressure on our decision.

A Recapitulating Metaphor of Sin

The evil which one person suffers results not from
blind forces, nor from a jokester God, but from decisions in which we all partake. Each suffers from and is
himself moved to sin. Here are the beginnings of the
notion of "sinful social structures." We need to reflect
on this experience more closely, in the light of the biblical tradition outlined above, in order to arrive at one or
another recapitulating metaphor which will be helpful.
Why recapitulating metaphor? The normal expectation
is that we achieve a concept, a definition which would
pull together in a meaningful pattern the threads of our
experience.

All indications are, however, that sin is not amena-
ble to direct analysis. It cannot be defined by a coherent, unified conceptual scheme. It is, as I outlined earlier, opaque. It makes no sense. Paul Ricoeur has
developed a helpful language. Freedom, he says, admits
of "pure description" when dealt with abstractly. We
can discover and describe directly the structures of freedom. But when we must deal with the cruel facts of sin,
we find only a "coded language" which speaks indirect-

ly, through metaphor, symbol and seeming contradiction.[4]

We are dealing with the general human ambiguity and with the special opacity of sin. I shall explore these briefly to show how a recapitulating metaphor can be of help. Then I shall develop a metaphor which I think will give some meaning to "sinful social structures."

When I dwelt on Pascal's image of "disproportion," I was in effect speaking about general human ambiguity. Human beings are "spiritual," that is, they have a thirst for overarching coherence. But they are "material," that is, they must painstakingly piece together the coherence they seek with fragments of reality which they have at their disposal during the fragments of time available. They are called to freedom, to embrace freely and lovingly all good, and ultimately to enter into union with God. But they can do this only by opting among the finite concrete things and people in their lives. Men are capable of understanding all things; yet they must puzzle over one situation after another, come to some understanding of it and then try to pull their insights together into coherent wholes: concepts, models, paradigms.

Perhaps the language of some contemporary philosophers is more helpful. They speak of the need to effect the transition from "objectivity to existence." A person first finds himself in the world among objects; he must learn, through dealing with objects both purposively and reflectively, to respect other selves; interacting with them, he will come to self-possession in freedom.

As I tried to make clear earlier, the possibility of evil emerges within that rift. The process of gathering oneself is heartbreakingly slow. It can take place only through both constant reflection about one's own interiority and constant exploration of the possibilities inherent in the circumstances around one. Many of these possibilities are beguiling even though they do not square with a long series of commitments already made. Coherence, depth, fidelity—sometimes these qualities seem to be only fancy words for stubbornness or even for fear of new things. We tend to lose heart and turn to the partial consolations which are at least at hand.

But lurking behind these blandishments is the special opacity of evil. For to choose evil is to choose darkness over light, death over life, chaos over coherence. What sense can it make that a man engage the apex of his being, his freedom, in an enterprise to undermine and destroy that very freedom, that very being?

This senselessness gives rise to the bitter remorse which is a quality of the language of confession. We read in Psalm 51 or in the Parable of the Prodigal Son the remorse of a serious man looking back upon his sinful decision.

> Then he came to his senses and said, "How many of my father's paid servants have more food than they want, and here am I dying of hunger! I will leave this place and go to my father and say: Father, I have sinned against heaven and against you; I no longer deserve to be called your son; treat me as one of your paid servants" (Lk. 15, 17-20).

There is bewilderment as well as horror with oneself: how could I have done it? Given the choice between evil and good, between nothing and all, it is the mystery of darkness itself that a person should freely sin.

This bewilderment with which a person looks back on sin gives rise to reflection about the moment of sinful decision itself. In what sense does anyone have "full knowledge" or give "full consent"? At that moment it is the experience of being tempted, of being swayed which is paramount. Is "sin" ever a word which a person uses at the moment of deciding: "I hereby sin"? Do we not always have speciously good motives, as well as the real one? "Sin" is a judgmental word, a word we use about a past decision from which we now dissociate ourselves. It *now* is seen to have been a senseless, destructive choice, even though *then* it seemed to have been perfectly reasonable. In confessing sin, a man tries to shine light on the darkness of that moment.

The Metaphor of "Slave-Will"

Paul Ricoeur develops the symbol of the slave-will as suggestive of the opaque mystery of human sin. Luther was the first to use this paradox. Augustine had coined the word "liberum arbitrium" (literally, "free will") to denote men's ability freely to sin. Augustine had wanted to reserve the word "libertas" (literally, "freedom") for that freedom which is exercised to answer yes to God's call and be fulfilled in love. Augustine wanted to highlight the savage irony that this very same freedom could be exercised in such a way that man's very being would be subverted. Hence a different term for the freedom to sin. Luther took the paradox and built it right into the words. He spoke of a "servum arbitrium," of a slave-will, of "a free will which is bound and which always finds itself already bound."[5]

This metaphor is best expounded by re-enacting the moment of repentance, of confession. It is at this moment that a person first brands the decision a "sin." The decision, when first made, seemed to fit right into the pattern of the person's life, seemed to make enough sense, contributed substantially (for I am here speaking of a serious decision) to the building story which tells who a person is. But now, at the moment of repentance, a different light is cast on that past event, for now a different "story" is emerging, a different person is being put together. Now the person looks back on that decision with horror, with sorrow, with bewilderment: how could I have done that?

The person is clearly accepting responsibility: he is confessing guilt. The act of repentance—itself a free act, constitutive of personhood—is reaffirming the person-constituting freedom of the earlier act. But the exercise of freedom is not enough to answer the shocked question, "How could I have done that?" The bewilderment leads the person to recognize that before the decision, the evil was outside, powerful, fascinating, terrifying, in a word, tempting.

The woman you gave me for a companion, she gave me fruit from the tree, and I ate it (Gen. 3, 12).

The serpent tricked me, and I ate (Gen. 3, 13).

In the moment of confession a person recognizes himself as having been "in a situation" which was not neutral. He insists that he was "captivated" by the temptation . . . *but this captivation became captivity only because it was freely willed.*

This freely willed captivity is not remote from everyday life. Take, for instance, the blacks' struggle for their rights and their identity, which was my first example of a contemporary crisis in Chapter 1. How many people have refused blacks entry to their shop or office, saying "I have nothing against them; it's just that if I let them in, I'll lose all my other business." The person who says that is not only captive of social opinion, but he also contributes freely to his own and others' captivity.

Often the language of confession uses the metaphor of defilement, of the need to be cleansed. This metaphor again brings out the power of evil when still external. Evil impinges upon the person, sullying him. But the defilement, at the moment of the sinful decision, ceases to impinge from the outside. It becomes internalized, part of the sinner himself.

Wash away all my guilt
and cleanse me from my sin (Ps. 51, 2).

This metaphor of "freedom in captivity" cannot be understood to be the picture of a man who has been, through an earlier decision, put into a jail and now would like out but cannot escape. That might adequately describe a man who makes a mistake and must suffer physical consequences: a man tries a foolhardy stunt, breaks his leg. Though he might regret his foolishness the cast does not go away. He must "do his time" until the leg mends. This is not the state of the sinner: all the time the sinner is in bondage it is a *bondage freely willed.* Sin is an act of freedom freely in captivity. This is of course, paradoxical. What I have been doing is spinning out the basic metaphor so that the absurdity of evil comes to light. The metaphor thus brings out both the power of sin and the freedom of the sinner.

Another Metaphor: "Knowingly Ignorant"

Ricoeur has sought balance right at the heart of evil: balance between man's ethical freedom and man's tragic passivity, between the nothingness and the power of sin. I hope now to develop another symbol, that of a person knowingly choosing to remain ignorant or cherishing illusions. Neither of these metaphors is right or wrong. Each is in its own way helpful.

I hope to show in another way that evil has power as well as being empty. At the same time I hope to probe further into the biblical data about all men's complicity in sin. In this way I hope to fill out what might be meant by "sinful social structures."

I get the language for this metaphor primarily from Bernard Lonergan who contrasts the love of light with the love of darkness.[6] Lonergan wishes to reserve a special word "scotosis" for the unconscious process of blocking understanding. But quite apart from that operation of the censor, there is the deliberate (by now we have some understanding of the complexity of the word) choice to abandon certain lines of inquiry and pursue others, to adopt certain perspectives and exclude others. People insist that certain problems are important, that others are trivial. St. Thomas Aquinas roots evil in the same choice of the narrow, short-term perspective over the broad, long-term perspective.[7] Aquinas says that "the will is the cause of evil only inasmuch as it is deficient," that is, when it "proceeds to

election without consideration of rule or measure."[8]
Lonergan has, with his usual sharply etched style, expanded on this idea.

> What is basic sin? It is the irrational. Why does it occur? If there were a reason, it would not be sin. There may be excuses; there may be extenuating circumstances; but there cannot be a reason, for basic sin consists, not in yielding to reasons and reasonableness, but in failing to yield to them . . .

> . . . basic sin is not an event; it is not something that positively occurs; on the contrary, it consists in a failure of occurrence, in the absence in the will of a reasonable response to an obligatory motive.

> . . . Besides what is positively and what simply is not, there is the irrational constituted by what could and ought to be but is not.[9]

People do not think through all the consequences of their actions; they concentrate on one or other aspect of a proposed course of action. They do not wait for all the evidence to see if their reading of a situation is adequate. But they do act. The basis for their action is partially reasonable, partly irrational—either from ignorance or malice. I wish to explore the source of the irrationality and the consequences. The source are "biases." The consequence is a further encroachment by irrationality of the historical process, leading some other people to further destructive and defensive moves, and others to be crushed.

Bias

The business of living is to a great extent the building up of an autobiography, a story which tells who a
person is. Man's freedom, his self-possession, his ability
to love are not so much gifts (except in a theological
sense) as tasks. Each of us begins life without freedom:
babies are completely subject to biological constraints;
it is only over many years that children can learn to
broaden their horizons past the instant meeting of biological and emotional needs. We all spend our lives in a
burgeoning (or diminishing) exercise of freedom, trying
to achieve at least a workable self-possession and
peace.

In this process, people make decisions about what
sort of person they want to be. These decisions are
made under many influences; they are made at least in
part quite unconsciously—or at least implicitly. But
there emerges a set of values, of images, of roles which
a person considers appropriate and operative for him.
Now, it can easily happen that circumstances will arise
which, to an objective bystander, make it clear that the
role or the self-image which a person has adopted is in-
appropriate or even destructive. For instance, a young
man who has spent years developing the self-image of a
gruff, brusque he-man ought to find this behavior inap-
propriate with his wife or his young children. It is possible for him to recognize this; it is also possible to overlook the newness of his present situation and the
inappropriateness of the old patterns. This oversight
can be unconscious, neurotic; but it can also be a choice
to so read the situation that one's earlier self-under-
standing remains intact. Individual bias is the refusal to

grow and the consequent refusal to recognize new demands on one's person.

When an individual acts on the basis of bias, he often receives stronger signals which he cannot overlook. For instance, our brusque young man might well overlook his wife's unspoken pleas—or even her verbal complaints—that he be more sensitive to her feelings. But chances are that his wife will eventually express her feelings of being neglected in other ways (for instance, she might leave him), ways which he cannot ignore for they undermine the image of himself which he has still been building. Individual biases are, then, somewhat fragile.

On the other hand, if a person finds or is part of a group which shares his values and reinforces his image of himself, that group will also reinforce his biases. Group bias is much tougher, much more resistant to light.

There are myriad examples of group bias. Interest groups are clearly formed simply to protect biases. Class is a notion which has clear reference to quite permanent interest groups. To share in group bias is to pursue only those avenues of investigation or reflection which tend to bolster the prestige or power of the group. It is to ignore or to discount or to suppress understanding of any truth which might reveal the group's well-being to the excessive or its usefulness at an end. Group bias is at the heart of the illusions which have led to the crises mentioned in Chapter 1. For instance, most people in mainstream North America firmly believe that blacks and welfare recipients are lazy.

Besides group bias, Fr. Lonergan also speaks of "general bias." He lays this to the impatience of common sense, which is concerned with the concrete and pragmatic.

It is easily led to rationalize its limitations by engendering a conviction that other forms of human knowledge are useless or doubtfully valid.[10]

It seems that general bias is part of the inbuilt conservatism of any culture. Continuity and stability are, after all, among the highest values of any society. Each society has a certain form of common sense and of conventional wisdom. It resists challenges to this common sense, for it resists change. This means that it resists recognizing its limitations.

But this is precisely what I meant in Chapter 1 by the historical illusions which eventually lead to crisis. For example, there are general biases, shared by rich and poor alike which are operative in the crises mentioned in Chapter 1. It was assumed generally (perhaps no longer) that the forms of political democracy developed in North America are superior to all others and that other forms should be "contained"—by war if necessary. It is also assumed that the affluence of North America is the best proof of our superior culture and that the growth of this affluence should remain our highest priority. (I shall explore this last bias in the next chapter.)

Right now I am developing the metaphor for sin of "knowing ignorance." Biases are the source of the irrationality which is, within the framework of this metaphor, the heart of sin. I wish next to explore the consequences of this irrationality, that is, the dynamics of bias. But to do this, we need first to understand the importance of "situation" in our exercise of freedom.

The Structuring of Situations

I think it is clear, as we progress from the discussion of individual bias to group bias to general bias, that at each level the action based on bias has more chance of distorting the subsequent situation. One egocentric husband does not have the power to impose his version of reality on his wife. But classes do; and, even more so, society does. We need to explore the mechanisms by which situations are structured and often distorted by those with power.

I must, first of all, make more precise what I mean by "situation." I find it helpful to make a difference between circumstances and situation. I would understand circumstances to be all the factors which are "not me" and over which a person has no control, but which impinge on him. On the other hand, situation includes the subject. It connotes interaction. It includes those factors in a person's circumstances with which he is prepared to deal, of which he is conscious, concerning which he is deciding.

If a person were perfectly objective and understood all things, then his situation would be as complex and balanced as his circumstances. But human knowledge is limited, and every person is biased. Hence each situation is never more than a part of circumstances; and usually a distortion.

Because men live in time and place, all acts of freedom are exercised within a situation. Freedom is never abstract; it is always with respect to a situation. For this very reason, the situation delimits and restricts the scope of freedom. For a decision is made only in terms of the challenge of a given situation. And, while, as I have shown above, a person can exercise some freedom in the structuring of the situation, the experience is always that the situation was "already there" when the person entered it. It is experienced as structured. According to this value-laden, affect-laden structure, the situation influences the freedom of the person.

Persons *interact* with situations. More precisely, persons interact and their interaction is structured and channeled by the situation in which they find themselves. We follow the example of people we meet, since we find them likeable or admirable. Others we find somewhat threatening or at least unlikeable; we take steps to keep them at a distance. They in turn receive these affect-laden signals and react. At the same time, both parties can be affected by other surroundings: the beauty or bleakness of the physical ambiance, the weather, etc. The situation is structured; the person, through earlier commitments, is structured. For this reason there is interaction.

There is a similar dialectical interaction in each situation between an individual and society itself. Most of the factors in a situation, no matter how private and intimate, are structured by society. It will strike many careful readers as an unwarranted personalization to use "society" as the agent of an action. Such usage must be justified. The sociology of knowledge is a theoretical attempt to understand this process whereby knowledge, attitudes, and behavior are socially distributed.[11]

In the business of daily living, people must learn to cope with problems. The identification and solution of problems is a social, cooperative enterprise. Since we would find it a waste of time to reinvent the wheel each generation, we find it normal that each generation teach the next about problems and their solutions. So we are taught to identify general patterns of behavior in others. (Sociologists call these patterns institutions.) And we are taught typical satisfactory responses to institutional patterns. (These are known as roles.) What begins as a satisfactory way to deal with problems, such as insuring the food supply, quickly becomes a kind of dance. Each person in a community has been taught to expect certain behavior from others and to respond appropriately. This provides everyone with a stable social order with a minimum of emotional and intellectual agonizing each day about what should be done.

The individual has no experience of having taken part in constructing "the way things are." He simply finds situations structured. Indeed, society is encountered as massively intractable, as objective. But this objectivity is constructed by men; it has its roots in the behavior of men who are acting out decisions based on their understanding of problems.

Here it becomes clear how limited is the exercise of any individual's freedom, how the structuring of the situation by the decisions of generations of his forerunners restricts his scope.

First, there are the expectations of his contemporaries to consider. They will be outraged if he breaks the established order of things and does not behave in accordance with the roles assigned him. In one way or another they will punish him: for even their disapproval and withdrawal will usually be bitter punishment. Social pressure, then, will influence behavior heavily.

But it is not simply behavior which is modified. The common stock of knowledge which dictates people's understanding of "how things are" is assumed to be all there is to know.

. . . the particular social world becomes the world
tout court. What is taken for granted as knowledge
in the society comes to be coextensive with the
knowable, or at any rate provides the framework
within which anything not yet known will come to
be known in the future.[12]

It is unthinkable for most men to behave any other
than the way prescribed; reality itself is limited to that
which everyone thinks it is. (This is the "general bias.")

For if there is to be a stable social order, there
must be more provided for people than prescribed behavior. These role prescriptions must be legitimated,
rationalized. These need to be more than convenient
ways to solve everyday problems. They need coherence.
Enmeshed in the practical knowledge about problems
and the consequent role prescriptions, enmeshed in the
language used to hand on these traditions is a *symbolic
universe of meaning*. The configuration of roles, the
division of labor, is all seen to make sense. Since these
social realities comprise the reality of life, the overarching canopy of meaning which is their framework gives
meaning to life. Men not only order their lives prag-
matically through social order, they provide each other
with safeguards against the ultimate terror, the night-
mare of chaos.[13] This, then, is the ultimate restraint
over freedom which forms the background, the framework of every situation. The individual who casts aside
the agreed-upon structures will have to face isolation
and the ultimate terror of meaninglessness. It takes a
very strong-minded person to be sure that he, and not
the others, is in touch with reality.

So it is easy enough to understand how "socialization" works, that is, the process whereby the individual

appropriates the values and perceptions of those who form his community. This acceptance is so thorough that it passes for common sense. The world taken for granted by the group is the only world: it is reality itself.

Dynamic of Bias

If an individual acts on the basis of egocentric bias, the consequences will probably be quite painful for him. He is not able to make his biases real. But when many people form a group on the basis of bias or when everyone within a community agrees, then their bias has the power to distort subsequent social reality. Their bias will structure the subsequent situations of themselves and others. An irrational element has been introduced into the social situation. This element is destructive: destructive of coherence, of meaning, of well-being, perhaps even of life. But once it is there, it will provoke not a reversal of the irrational but an accumulation of the irrational.[14] For if there were a circle of trust among all men, then the situation in which each found himself would call for an open, loving, generous response. But once that circle is broken, once the earliest structures are those of contest, and distrust and domination, then the situation invites each person to respond defensively. The roles we are taught are meant not only to channel our contribution to society, they are meant to help us protect ourselves. We learn early to act on the basis of our own biased insights into a situation—a bias toward protecting our own personal interests. This in turn further skews the subsequent situation, provoking others to still further defensive action.

The dark seems powerful enough to overcome the light.

Bias, narrow self-interest, defensiveness, short-sightedness—these qualities are all dynamic qualities. They tend to overcome their opposites.

When a society provides mechanisms for transmitting skills and roles to its young, we can then ask whether these skills are distributed equally. I can put the question in another way. The community transmits skills to cope with everyday problems. In a society so complex as ours, *whose problems* are being handled in the process of socialization? If social power is coercive ultimately not by exacting appropriate behavior, but by convincing that reality itself cannot be otherwise, does the exercise of social power today show up in the sorts of biases which, for instance, form the basis of the educational system?

Sinful Social Structures

Let us pause and see where we are. We began this chapter with a study of the biblical reflection on the power of sin. We experience this power when tempted. St. John's usage of "world" brings out that men experience both their inescapably personal responsibility for evil and the power of evil in social interaction. The metaphor of "servile-will" brings out the opaque mystery of the tension between freedom and the power of evil. The metaphor of "knowing ignorance" has helped to unravel how men's social interaction affects the freedom of each by structuring situations.

We have been trying to work away from a simplistic notion of the "full knowledge" and "full consent" required in order to speak of sin. At the dark moment of decision it seems that it is the allurement and power of evil which is paramount; it is only later, in the moment of conversion, that a person recognizes, to his bitter remorse, that he was personally, freely responsible.

It is similarly opaque in the interplay between reasonableness, the long view, and generosity on the one hand and the irrational, the short term, and the egocentric on the other. These latter can seem the only prudent course; only later do they reveal their true colors. "How could I?" is the bewildered cry of the repentant man. While there is no reasonable answer, we have nonetheless explored what meaning can be derived.

This we have done by noticing the dynamics of bias: when once acted upon and especially when once agreed upon, the comfortable oversight or the rationalized infidelity distorts subsequent situations, evoking not its reversal but an accumulation of the irrational, a widening of the circle of mistrust. People expect the worst of others and prepare for it by accumulating power. Biases are built into everyday practices. Inequality becomes characteristic of the most basic social structures.

A social structure can then be meaningfully said to be sinful. It can be sinful in its source: a social structure emerges as people act out a decision which is biased, narrow and destructive. It can be sinful in its consequences: others confronted with a situation so structured are provoked to react defensively and so to reinforce the destructive characteristics of the situation. Still other people, lacking the power to react defensively, will experience sharp limitations on their effective scope of freedom and hence will experience the structures as offensive to their human dignity.

The Present Disillusion (Reprise)

In Chapter 1, I spoke of the contemporary crises which are now emerging. I suggested that to face these crises, people would have to shed historic illusions. The fundamental illusion to be shed, I argued, was that evil is one more technical problem. In this chapter I have tried to show that the traditional Christian notion of sin can be understood to be operative in society. I now can be more specific about the illusions which are resulting in crises today.

What kind of society could be expected to emerge, once the consensus was reached that the scientific method alone would shape our culture's relation to reality? Human values needed for community such as fidelity and trust were excluded from meaningful public discussion, for the prosaic mind demanded clarity and "objectivity." Only quantitative criteria were publicly accepted. An ethic of growth was adopted.

In the name of better management and increased benefit for all, a key abstraction was made—the economic abstraction. A scientific model, first worked out by Adam Smith and constantly improved over the past 200 years, showed that by competition society could most efficiently husband its scarce resources and maximize economic growth.

The decision, arrived at over a long period in our society, seems at one level to have been a beneficial one. Yet it is my contention that it is the most fundamental example of a social sin. It has led to a set of social structures which breed mistrust and enhance inequality. Until we in North America face this mistrust and this inequality, we will only pick at the edges of the social problems which are reaching the critical stage.

What is happening in North America today? One group, the middle-class mainstream, are transmitting the message, in accordance with the dominant symbol system of North American society: "Be a winner." The children in "better" schools receive it, along with a schooling in the skills needed to be a proficient consumer and producer and in competitive attitudes. Their parents receive it through advertising, through the pressure put on them by peers to attain the trappings of success, through hiring and promotion procedures which stress certain skills and attitudes.

Another group, comprised of the racial minorities, of the poor, of the retarded, are beamed another message: "You're a loser." Their children receive it in slum schools. The adults receive it from employment offices, credit agencies, welfare workers, policemen, shop clerks —from everyone in the mainstream. It quickly becomes a self-fulfilling prophecy, a structure imposed on every situation they enter.

People in the mainstream find their situation so structured that they are pressed to opt for managerial, competitive, ambitious self-images. The poor minority find their situation so structured that they experience blocks to their freedom economically, culturally and even politically. Each group encounters evil; that is, forces destructive of coherence in their lives, destructive of growth toward full, generous love, destructive of their human dignity.

My contention is that this evil is moral in origin. People—rich and poor alike—are daily encountering social structures which are sinful, rooted in sinful (i.e., biased, narrow, destructive) decisions. The mainstream majority suffer from the sinfulness of these situations and are the very ones who share the responsibility.

They are freely in bondage: they have chosen to be sub-
servient to social forces unleashed by their own value
choices. They are knowingly ignorant: the pain of their
situation is evident to them, but they refuse to see the
connection between the pressures they undergo and the
assumptions they make about society.

There is in our society a need to be forgiven—
publicly. If the present crises are to be faced creatively,
basic assumptions which narrow our perception of the
problems must be questioned. The task of shattering
illusions must be undertaken with the hope to rebuild, a
hope engendered only by the assurance of forgiveness.

My view, I am sure, runs counter to the perception
of society which most readers have. Do I exaggerate?
Has not North American society done more good than
harm? Or have we reached a point where it must be
said that the harm undermines all the good? Is a more
conservative stance simply the result of "bondage," of
"knowing ignorance"? I shall try to answer these questions in the next chapter by becoming more concrete.

ing to the responsibilities you had; there would then be good serfs and bad kings. Equality in the face of death, equality at the last judgment was what counted. The friezes in medieval cathedrals showing kings and popes in hell relativized the social inequalities; the possibility of serfs being saints lent each serf dignity.

But in contemporary society inequality has, on the basis of the most important myths, no meaning and no legitimation. For we are proudest of the fact that we are a democracy, where each has equal opportunity, regardless of race, color or creed. The brute fact of inequality is, therefore, ascribed to the victims themselves. The poor and the racial minorities are not down because anyone keeps them down—quite the contrary, all liberal-minded people want everyone up—but because they like being down. They refuse to adopt those attitudes, those living patterns which would insure that they would be like everyone else. Being poor becomes a vice, a deviation; being black becomes a vice, a deviation; speaking Spanish or French becomes a vice, a deviation—all in the name of equality.

Of all the inequalities which stem from injustice, I have chosen in this chapter to concentrate on poverty. Perhaps this case is the most complex; but for that very reason it brings out the cruel fraud of how the system preaches equality for all, yet, in the words of the Canadian Senate Report on poverty, ". . . not only tolerates poverty, but also creates, sustains and even aggravates it."[2] No individual person, I am sure, maliciously wills the poverty of the poor. But almost every affluent American and Canadian is implicated in the poverty of others by sharing assumptions about man and the world, which, while they seem realistic and benign, actually result in inequality and poverty.

The Shape of Poverty

In subsequent sections I shall try to expand the notion of poverty, but for the moment I wish to dwell only on the quantitative aspects of poverty. I wish, in other words, to treat poverty as lack of income. While this perspective is limited, it has its own validity.

Estimates differ (depending on the exact definition of poverty adopted) but in the early '60's there were as many as 40 million poor in the U.S. and 5 million in Canada.[3] Yet even with so many poor in our midst, it took Michael Harrington's now famous book to jolt people into an awareness of poverty amid affluence.[4]

We in North America pride ourselves on the affluence which we have achieved. In 1964 the annual flow of goods and services (the Gross National Product, as it is called), measured in U.S. dollars was: United States: $3,290; Canada: $1,940; Ireland: $800; Mexico: $430; Bolivia: $140; India: $90.[5]

It is difficult for a person brought up in North America to imagine living on $800 a year. We begin to appreciate how relative is the term poverty when confronted with India. Everyone in North America—even the poorest—is relatively well off compared with the maimed beggars of Calcutta. For this reason it is not very meaningful to try to settle on a list of goods and services which gets defined as "subsistence" and to speak of those below that line as poor. I would rather concentrate on the *unequal distribution of income.*

This inequality seems to be impervious to the growing affluence of North America. Canadians and Americans have, on the average, become much richer in the past generation. Per capita personal income rose in the U.S. from $1870 in 1951 to $3410 in 1968; and in

Canada from $1130 in 1951 to $3100 in 1970. And yet
during roughly those same years the poorest fifth of the
U.S. population continued to receive only 5% (i.e., one
quarter of their share) of the total income.[6] In Canada,
the poorest fifth received 4.4% of the total income in
1951 and 4.6% in 1965.[7] Indeed, by 1971, the share of
the poorest fifth of Canadians had dropped to 3.6%.[8]
During those same years the richest fifth in both U.S.
and Canada received more than 40% of total income, or
more than twice their share.

There are many faces of poverty. I wish here only
to point to some of those statistics which most sharply
contradict general attitudes toward the poor.

In the U.S. in 1966, women outnumbered men 8 to
5 among the poor. Of women heading a family, no less
than 35% were poor. Of children without a father, 3 out
of 5 were being raised in poverty.[9] In Canada in 1967,
35.6% of all families headed by women were poor.[10]
The economic system in North America dispenses income through the mechanism of jobs. Women are dis-
criminated against in the labor market; women who
have children to tend have a second strike against them.

There is also a racial factor to poverty. In the
U.S., in 1963, 19% of white families were poor, while
48% of nonwhite families were poor.[11] We mentioned
that 35% of all families headed by women were poor;
53% of black families headed by women were poor.[12] It
has been estimated that over 85% of the Canadian Indi-
ans live in poverty.

Are the poor lazy? Of all heads of poor families in
the U.S., 56% work full time.[13]

In 1966, 1 in 4 poor families was headed by a man
who had worked throughout the year . . . All told

among poor families headed by men under age 65, 5 out of 6 of the heads worked some time in 1966, and the majority of those who didn't were disabled.[14]

In Canada about 70% of the poor cannot work, because they are either old or disabled or women who must stay home with children.[15]

A "poverty gap" has been calculated, comprising the aggregate difference between the actual income of the poor and the income they would require for human dignity. For the U.S. in 1965, it was $11 billion; for Canada in 1969 it was $2.7 billion.[16] This is some measure of the inequality in our system: a tiny amount when compared with the U.S. military budget, yet a crushing burden for the millions of poor.

Poverty as Unequal Participation in Society

The affluence of modern-day North America depends upon a vast, complex technology which has been developed. This technology demands of people that they learn highly specialized skills and depend upon others to learn equally narrow skills. A web of interdependence has emerged more than ever before. While most Americans and Canadians still live out of the folklore of individualism, *participation* in the complexity of the technical society has become the key to affluence, to dignity, to freedom.

To be free is no longer a matter of removal of restraints in individual initiative. To be free now means being empowered by the society to participate. This is the significance of the new preoccupation with participation.[17]

Furthermore, in our society money is the means whereby people have access to all the societal goods and services, to the skills and attitudes necessary to enjoy the benefits of the affluence.

These skills and attitudes are cultural benefits, which, along with more material benefits, are distributed unequally. In the concrete, each member of society receives these benefits through institutions—family, school, hospital, government bureaus, police, the courts. A second level at which to view poverty is to see it as the systematic exclusion of certain people from these institutional benefits.

It is the exclusion of low-income people (from the broader social and economic participation which is open to others), when this exclusion is not voluntary on their part, which we define as being the essence of poverty.[18]

Public policies which find expression through major institutions of Canada and the U.S. are such that the poor are excluded from their benefits—not because lawmakers and bureaucrats are evil, but because the poor are poor.

The poor are at a significant disadvantage in the labor market. They find it harder to get jobs; they earn less when working; they have fewer opportunities for occupational training and upgrading; they are more prone to be laid off or fired. Lack of skills, poor education, malnutrition and poor health, lack of information about available jobs—these frustrate the poor when they seek employment. If they do find a job, it is most often in an occupation which is not organized, for instance, in the service industries or with a small manufacturing firm. Thus they are likely to receive lower wages than organized workers. For instance, in Canada manpower policy is supposedly aimed at upgrading the labor force, but programs are so set up that it is difficult for the very needy to qualify; instead, those who have already attained a moderate level of skills form the main group of clientele.

The poor are at a disadvantage in the consumer market. Their lack of education and of money means they have less access to the kind of information needed for efficient buying. They often lack means of transportation, so they cannot do comparative shopping. Their inability to amass any money to buy ahead means they cannot buy larger quantities at better prices. Prices are therefore higher in the chain store outlets in the slums; prices are higher there the day the welfare checks come. The poor pay more.

Nor do the poor have access to credit in times of need or to buy more efficiently. They have unstable incomes and few assets; the banks and even the credit unions consider them too bad a risk. So they are forced to go to the finance companies where they pay exorbitant—usurious—interest rates. If they are unable to pay, their notes are refinanced time and again, until their payments become little more than tribute money; often they have forgotten what it was they bought.

It is also more difficult for the poor to benefit from the schools. Research has shown that the experiences of a very young child in a deprived environment may hamper his future development. Once in the school system, the progress of poor children tends to be slower, their grades lower, and their drop-out rate higher than for children from other homes.[19] The "loser" attitude is ingrained early—parents and teachers alike ingrain it.

With respect to housing, the poor again suffer. Inadequate housing can lead to family disruption and despair, ill-health and disease. Yet housing policy has in both Canada and the U.S. consistently failed to meet the needs of the poor.[20] Based on a "trickle-down" theory (which said that as the affluent got better houses, they would vacate their old houses, leaving them for poorer households), housing policies have, for the most part, helped those who could help themselves. The provision of public housing has been grossly inadequate. For those who have been able to live in public housing, administrative rules have often provided another source of discrimination. For example, by increasing rents dollar-for-dollar with any increase in income the household may earn, the possibility of increasing the family standard of living is eliminated. Privacy and stability of tenure have often not been guaranteed, rights which are not questioned for private housing.

Before the law at least, the poor—so one would think—receive equal treatment. But the statistics reveal a great imbalance. The overwhelming majority of those convicted of crime are from among the poor. One is led to suspect that the majority of Canadians and Americans associate poverty with crime, success with respectability. Thus the definition of crimes in the Criminal Code and the enforcement of law, both of which reflect the attitudes of the majority, tend to reflect the notion that criminality is a social "disease" and acceptable only among those who are already social misfits. The dominant group tends to affirm its respectability; they can face poverty with complacency.

There are other examples of this systematic exclusion of the poor from society's basic benefits, notably in the provision of health services.

The Vanier Institute concludes its brief on poverty:

The picture that emerges from the limited information above is one of two different Canadas, made different not by virtue of different institutions but by institutions which operate differently for different users. Canada Major is a country of reasonable optimism and some expectation of security, of rising real standards of living, and of physical and social needs which are likely to be met. In Canada Minor what emerges suggests insecurity, particularly the insecurity associated with unemployment and hence income interruption. There is also fear, and an expectation of failure rather than success. Physical deprivation and social exclusion are often anticipated and experienced. Optimism in Canada Major and fear and alienation in Canada Minor constitute rational responses to the environment in each country. Citizens transported from one to the other find more than their income altered by the change. . . .

On the basis of limited but rather persuasive evidence, it appears that the current policies of our institutions may be maintaining poverty in Canada or at the very least delaying its elimination. It also appears that to the degree that the poor have characteristics which differ from those of the non-poor, some part of this difference is likely to be attribu-

table to the more unpleasant experiences they have
accumulated in the environment in which they live.
To ask them to change *in the absence of environ-
mental change* is to ask for irrationality on their
part.[21]

While the prevailing attitudes of the majority of
Canadians and Americans do not imply any explicit
malice on the part of individuals, nonetheless the poor
are *systematically* excluded from the benefits of this society.

Poverty as Lack of Power

What I mean by power is implicit in the discussion
of the last chapter. It is the ability to influence events.
It is not simply the ability to coerce the behavior of
another; it is much more the ability to shape situations,
even to distort them according to one's particular perspective. In a broad sense, society holds ultimate
power, simply because the agreed-upon and taken-for-
granted interpretation of reality and prescription of behavior is taken by almost all to be the only reality and
the only way of doing things. But it is also true that
within society certain groups acquire the power to
shape events by shaping the perspectives and thereby
the behavior of almost all.

There are in society such realities as an Underclass
and an Overclass. Because the Underclass has no
power, it cannot influence the situation of the Overclass. So the Overclass need not pay much attention to
the Underclass. The Overs are able to read each situation in terms of their own aspirations and needs.[22]

When they hear the cries of frustration and anger they are often genuinely puzzled: are they not grateful for what they have? their excessive demands bespeak their lack of civilization! Industrial workers were treated with this reaction until they organized. Blacks still are. So are French Canadians. And so are the poor.

On the other hand, the Underclass must learn to read every possible message which comes from the Overclass, even though they are often foreign to them. The world of the ghetto child is hemmed in by the symbols and agents of the dominant group: police, teachers, television advertising. Each brings stern messages about the demands of the Overclass and about the exclusion and punishment meted out to those who fail. (Perhaps the most striking example of this asymmetrical flow of communication, depending on who has the power, is the state of bilingualism in Canada. Constitutionally, Canada is bilingual. What this has traditionally meant, however, is that French Canadians have had to learn English in order to "get ahead." And this has meant not just the language, but the attitudes and values of the alien but dominant majority.)

It is clear, then, that the poor lack power. Society is operated according to a different perspective than theirs; it is organized to meet other needs than theirs. The poor are not poor because they want to be poor. They are not poor because "that's the way things are." They are poor because others have the power which they do not have; and others exercise that power to their own benefit and to the detriment of the poor.

For the most part, Americans and Canadians are uneasy about talk of power, unequally shared, of the strong dominating the weak, of unwillingness to give up an advantage once acquired. This sort of talk about power and inequality and dominance runs counter to the cherished belief in innocence which we have inherited from the eighteenth century (discussed in Chapter 2). If there are flaws in society, so the belief goes, they are due to fear and ignorance. Enlightened self-interest, channelled by competition, will work to the good of all. We have only technical problems to solve: "If we can put together the team to put a man on the moon, surely we can work together to solve the problems of our cities." Thus, inequality is seen as just one more technical problem.

People prefer to think that the poor are poor because of a set of inevitable economic laws; or if pushed, because of the statistical inevitability that some people are less bright, less ambitious, less well organized. Talk of power, they feel, is going too far. It smacks of pernicious communist influence, or at least reflects a simple-minded conspiracy theory where vague words like "establishment" get thrown around.

To leave power out of one's account of social realities, to overlook how fiercely men strive to acquire dominance and how ruthlessly they exercise power in order to keep it—such simple faith in humanity can be dangerous. Here I return to what I believe is the essential contribution which a Christian, imbued with a realization of man's sinfulness and God's forgiving love, can make to the contemporary discussion about the crisis of our civilization. For the Christian can take these ugly realities into account.

This should enable him to *listen to the poor* as they organize and find their public voice. There is a sense in which the humanity of many poor people has been damaged: often circumstances have impaired their ability to make their way in economic, cultural and public life. A Christian's vision of social reality ought to help him hear the anger and frustration of the poor as they react to the treatment they are accorded. Further, a Christian vision of the fullness of humanity and of social evil should enable him to recognize the rich humanity of so many poor. They cannot express their humanity publicly the way mainstream North America does: through power, competition, consumption. They often have developed other qualities which get overlooked by our culture. A Christian must, therefore, learn to hear them not simply as people damaged by social structures but as people richly endowed with qualities and with insights unattainable by those who have learned, almost as a second nature, successfully to compete.

Many poor people attain a peace, a freedom, a dignity unknown to most affluent people. But this does not exonerate the affluent, who contribute to the straitening circumstances of those poor who are serene. In Solzhenitsyn's great novel, *First Circle*, it is the prisoners who are free men and the jailers who are in bondage. But this does not make the jailers any less unjust for imprisoning them.

Similarly, a reflective reading of Paolo Freire's *Pedagogy of the Oppressed* leads one to realize that the oppressor is not necessarily any more free than the oppressed. But while the oppressed can do little publicly (i.e., politically or economically) to alleviate the bondage of the oppressor, the oppressor must be held responsible for the conditions of bondage of the oppressed. Attempts to strip the poor of their human dignity usually fail; but they are nonetheless sinful.

Two questions remain.

1. How is it that the dominant, affluent majority have been able to ignore the evident exclusion of the

poor from social benefits, despite the evident humanity of the poor? I wish to develop an answer in terms of our recapitulating metaphor of sin: the plight and humanity of the poor is *knowingly ignored* by almost all members of this society in order to *cherish the illusion* that our choice of economic growth as the primary goal is a good and humanizing choice.

2. If the exclusion of the poor has been systematically overlooked, what has this done to the humanity of the affluent? I wish to develop the answer to this in terms of the other recapitulating metaphor of sin: the affluent mainstream remains *freely in bondage* to its economic vision of man and society.

The Illusion of the "Trickle-Down" Effect

Most people implicitly believe that there is a "trickle-down" effect. That is, they think that if a country continues to enjoy economic growth at the aggregate level, then this increasing wealth will eventually be distributed equitably and solve the problem of poverty. The statistics at the beginning of this chapter show that this just does not happen. Both Canada and the U.S. have grown at spectacular rates in the past 20 years, but there has been no substantial redistribution of income in the direction of equality or even of justice. The rich still get just about twice their share; the poor still get one-quarter their share.

Yet it is evident that uninterrupted maximization of economic growth is the highest priority in each country. Since the end of World War II governments in all the Western countries have undertaken, in the light of Keynes' analysis of the depression of the '30's, to assure full employment. This is taken to mean substantially the same thing as the highest possible economic growth.

The maximization of economic growth makes sense only if we live in a world of scarcity. The "economic vision" of reality was first forged in the eighteenth century, at a time when famine was a frequent recurrence and chronic hunger was the lot of the vast majority. At that time, the economic vision, blueprinting a method to marshal scarce resources in the most efficient way possible for the production of wealth, was seen as a liberation from one of men's oldest and most basic fears.

In the last generation, it has become clear that scarcity is not our problem in North America. The industrial machine can produce so much goods that there is a constant problem of having the goods bought. There is a constant pressure on jobs. Because our economic thinking runs in grooves worn deep over centuries, we still think of scarcity as our problem, and still want to solve all other problems by growth.

Hence there is still a national consensus in both Canada and the U.S. that the national goal must be more wealth: economic growth via increased productivity, increased technology. The outcome is the megamachine, a society based on the premise that more is better and that more technology, better applied, will magically solve our social ills, notably inequality.

Nationally, the sky is the limit. But perhaps the excessive garbage will someday indicate to North Americans that scarcity is not really our problem, that growth is not our solution; that there is, in fact, a maximum dictated by the limits of the environment itself. The next question is: will this experience of limitation become an ethical insight, capable of getting people to transform their perception of reality and then transforming basic institutional patterns?

Individually, unlimited acquisitiveness is encouraged by endless advertising. It is also condoned, for according to prevailing perceptions, society rewards people according to their contribution to cracking the problem of scarcity. People feel the money they "earn" to be theirs by right; their perception is that it has been their initiative, their inventiveness, their responsibility which have accounted for their getting ahead. They forget that in this highly complex, technological society nobody can accomplish anything alone.

I believe that we are here reaping one of the most tragic consequences of the decision, made I suppose in the eighteenth century, to become a "scientific" culture. Science, as I elaborated in Chapter 3, is based on abstractions. Science leaves out of account that which is not commensurable with the human mind, as it thrusts toward its goal of exhaustive explanation and unanimous consent. "Economic man" is such an abstraction. It leaves out most deeply human dreams and aspirations, human feelings and interactions. Because as a group we have decided that our society is an "economy," where our model is the factory, where persons have become "units of production" and "consumers," *we are left with no other criterion for choice than more growth*. We have as a people blinded ourselves, and knowingly continue to blind ourselves to any other dimension of the problem.

In order that this factory-world hang together the assumption has also been made that to be a fully responsible adult is the same as to work; and this in turn means "to have a job," to take part in the productive process.

That these assumptions are both outmoded and outrageous is indicated by the following practical consequences:

— at the aggregate level, we encourage socially irresponsible consumption and waste in order to "maintain jobs";

— we "develop human resources" in a "realistic" fashion to fit the pattern of jobs demanded by technology rather than developing jobs fit for people;

— at the personal level, we classify as "unemployable" (i.e. socially useless) those who cannot meet the demands of mobility raised by technology. They are typically rendered "immobile" by having too many children, by being "too old" (usually over 50), or by being unskilled. We systematically overlook the number of pleasant, creative and socially useful ways they could find to work if they were encouraged.

And of course the irony is that the technological mega-machine does not provide enough jobs. Our aim of maximum wealth means more capital-intensive means of production. Since jobs are the only means we have for distributing the income generated by production, the inequality will probably get worse, unless our vision of who we are is transformed.

The growth-machine which we have constructed continues to bring increased affluence to the comfortable mainstream. But it is so organized that it effectively excludes those who are deemed non-productive. It excludes them from benefits, from participating, and finally from any recognition of their human dignity. To use my language of Chapter 4, the dominant mainstream has so structured the situation of the poor minority that the scope of their freedom is drastically curtailed. For a long time the majority of the poor were so crushed that they did not protest. Now they have found their voice.

They are demanding, I would suggest, that we see beyond our economic abstractions. They are insisting that they too are mothers and fathers with deep feelings and aspirations for their children.

For the most part, we cannot hear what they say. What prevents us? We cannot see them as men and women, some hurting and angry, some crushed and despairing. Has our inability to recognize the poor anything to do with our own affluence and power? We never think of ourselves as either rich or powerful; but the vast majority are comfortable in a way no one in history has been. Do we refuse to hear the poor because we fear that it would lead to dismantling the system which serves us well? For, as I have tried to show, a real attack on inequality would mean more than increased welfare payments, more than just sharing what we have. It would mean transforming our system—and transforming our ideas and images of ourselves.

It seems to me that Americans and Canadians are, in their public life, refusing to face the moral challenge of inequality. Is this refusal sin? Can we use the excuse, "I didn't realize"? The poor are people; they are all around us; their protest has been made public. Sin is a mystery of darkness. Within that darkness, it has some meaning to say that we as communities have knowingly remained ignorant, we have cherished illusions. The treatment of the poor in both Canada and the U.S. is an example of "social sin."

Freely in Bondage to Our Own Economic Vision

The social and economic organization which we all help to maintain tends systematically to rob the poor of their humanity. Does it at least serve the humanity of the dominant majority? It seems to me that implicit in our culture's scientific—and by consequence economic —abstract view of man is dangerously narrow. This society's definition of success is based on that abstract, narrow vision. It is a notion of success that can be characterized as materialist. It overlooks some of men's basic needs. The benefits which "success" brings the modern North American tend to leave him—and especially her—empty.

Our society has concentrated on man as successful, man the dominator, the manipulator. But even the most successful among us falls prey to feelings of loneliness, of inadequacy, of doubt. Christianity—and the medieval society which was inspired by it—can put these experiences into a context which gives them meaning; it can speak of sacrifice, of suffering with Christ, suffering to build the mystical body with Christ victorious. But our society can only provide men with more techniques—psychology, drugs—with which to fend off unpleasant feelings. Men still get sick; men are still mortal. Christianity gives ultimate sense to these terrible experiences; modern society offers a man scientific medicine and a bedside manner, but cannot give meaning to the man's weakness. Modern society remains silent in the face of death.

This is the ambiguity of Western achievement. While it is true that the Western technological breakthrough has been in many respects a humanizing achievement, relieving the material suffering of millions, still the seeming endless drive to consume is rooted not in the satisfaction which material benefits bring, but in the torment of emptiness caused by these unexamined and unanswered questions.

Many ordinary people in North America feel this tension. They have spent a lifetime working hard. A house, a car, or two, a comfortable way of life are the results, and the only source of security and well-being that they know. Yet their children now tell them their life has been little more than a meaningless rat race; and they have begun to listen to this. Counter-cultural movements whose life-styles embody gentler values—such as friendship, reflectiveness and peace—strike chords in most of us. Big suburban houses isolate us from so many; machines set their own pace and disrupt the rhythms of reflection; success in work requires a hard edge. Yet will it help to move out, give away the car and lawn mower, quit the job?

The ambiguity gives rise to a further question. Can we speak of sin under the recapitulating metaphor of servile-will? Can we invoke the old natural law notion that history has its foreclosures, that if an act truly is sinful—destructive of humanity in both victim and perpetrator—then it contains the seeds of its own punishment? Have we, in freely, knowingly choosing to be blind to any other value being more important than economic growth, built a system to which we have freely enslaved ourselves?

The Western world made a cumulative, historical decision to become "economic," to amass wealth by the most efficient husbanding of scarce resources. The venture has been a success; but it has led the mainstream majority not only to comfort and lack of fear, but also into an endless round of consumerism. Is this so simply because, having produced all those goods, they now must buy them? It goes deeper than this.

To have opted to become economic implied opting to become "technic"; that is, to take on a very qualified relation to the world around us. Henceforth the dominant relation to nature would be not fear before her immense force, not awe before her delicate complex beauty, not reverence before her ability to lead to deeper mysteries; but manipulation, exploitation, mastery.

Charles Taylor, a political philosopher, has brilliantly sketched the implication of this choice:

. . . [the] self-image of modern industrial society [is that of] a vast productive engine based on creative work, disciplined and rational effort, and the division of labor.

. . . the cult of production projects a vision of man as dominating, transforming the surrounding world and enjoying the fruits of this transformation. It is because we place ultimate value on this form of human life that we are ready to make production the central function of modern society. But, in order to participate in this cult, individuals have to have some tangible part in the process of transforming/enjoying . . . (to be a consumer) is the only universally available mode of participation in the cult of production. Hence the poor in contemporary affluent societies suffer not just from material deprivation, but from a stigma. They are ex-communicated, as it were, from the dominant cult of modern society.

The drive to consumption is therefore no adventitious fad, no product of clever manipulation. . . . It is tied up with the economic self-image of modern society.[23]

This exploitative, manipulative attitude toward nature has historically gone hand in hand with modern Western man's self-image as entrepreneur, successful in the face of recalcitrant nature, successful in the face of clever competition. But the terror of measuring success through the consumption of material products is that the only benchmark of success can be invidious comparison. Since none of the gadgets is itself satisfying, the only source of satisfaction is knowing that others are less well off. The human emptiness of our competitive affluence and the persistence of poverty amid such plenty are two sides of the same coin. My two metaphors blend also: Western affluent man is freely in bondage because he persistently, knowingly blinds himself to any priority except economic growth.

6
Conclusion

It used to be that in old-fashioned sermons we heard that our materialism was tantamount to idolatry. What then seemed outrageously reactionary seems now, in the face of contemporary crises, to be frighteningly accurate. The great prophets not only condemn the sinfulness of idolatry, but jeer at its foolishness. The idolater consigns himself into servitude under a creature of his own hand. Modern man finds it hard to take seriously the bondage of the primitive idolater. But the enormous economic, social and political pressures which hem people in today are human products, created by human decisions. They can be changed, made more humanizing, by new human decisions—if we are willing to shift our assumptions, our goals, our priorities. The bondage which Western affluent man suffers is, in the end, of his own making.

In many ways this conclusion is, I am sure, unsatisfactory to most readers. It says at once too much and not enough. It will seem to many that my view of North American society is too harsh, too radical. Time alone will tell if the crises we now face are as deep as I think they are; and if they are essentially moral crises.

It is, of course, true that I have not said enough.

This is a small book, and meant to be a theological reflection. It is not primarily about social change. I have said nothing about how to decide which problems are the root problems. I chose domestic poverty as *an* example; I could have chosen many others: the problem of race at home and abroad; the widening gap between rich and poor nations; the use of economic and military power to perpetuate the gap between rich and poor; the rapidly emerging ecological problem. Those interested in social change have to hit upon criteria to determine which problems underlie others, which are more basic. I have not entered into this discussion at all.

Nor have I talked about strategy, about which problem to attack first, and how. Here an assessment must be made to see if people will be interested in a problem, and, if so, how apt the one problem will be to interest people in the whole skein of social problems. Often, for instance, those ready to do battle over a local issue show no interest in international questions; and those concerned about larger international issues won't get their hands dirty in local problems. Bridges have to be made, and are often best made by choosing the right starting point.

I have not dealt with the question whether to get directly involved in the political process in order to effect change, or whether to concentrate on longer term attitudinal change. Nor have I raised the question of where the institutional church should insert itself into the process of change.

Of what use, then, is theological reflection? It seems to me to be necessary in order to discover how deep the present problems are. Theological reflection has led me to find the mystery of evil at the root of contemporary social problems.

Thus, in my view, Christians are not being deflected from their essential mission when they take sides with the poor in our generation. They are proclaiming the mystery of God's forgiving love when they witness against the hard-hearted, narrowly focused common sense of our age, and insist on analyzing it in terms of how it treats the least of the brethren.

Nothing less than conversion is at stake. To be able to take the poor seriously, even when they are "troublemakers" and "radicals"; to be able to hear the voice of the "revolutionary," of the "terrorist" or "communist" in the Third World, is to be willing to redefine who we are. It entails transcending the horizons of our culture, breaking loose from the historical assumptions and perceptions which have molded us and told us who we are. To hear the voice of the poor is to receive, in other words, the grace of conversion.

Footnotes

INTRODUCTION

1. "Justice in the World," *The Pope Speaks*, vol. 16 (1972), p. 377. Italics mine.
2. *Ibid*. Italics mine.

CHAPTER 1

1. Cf. Bernard J. F. Lonergan, S.J., *Insight: A Study of Human Understanding*, New York: Philosophical Library, 1957, pp. 207-244. It will emerge that I am greatly influenced by Lonergan's thought; more specifically, chapter VII of *Insight* has been for years a guiding light.
2. G. Baum, "Contemporary American Romanticism: Response," *Concilium* V, May 1972, p. 137. Italics mine.
3. "Underdevelopment is a chronic state of violence": Denis Goulet, *The Cruel Choice*, New York: Atheneum, 1971, p. 317. The leading Latin American theologian of liberation is Gustavo Gutierrez, *A Theology of Liberation*, Orbis Books, Maryknoll, N.Y., 1973. For other references cf. Patrick Kerans, "Theology of Liberation," *Chicago Studies* XI, 2, Summer 1972, pp. 184-85.
4. In the language of H. Richard Niebuhr, while I note that Christ and culture can often stand in a relation of paradox, I believe finally in Christ, the transformer of culture. Cf. *Christ and Culture*, New York: Harper and Row (Harper Torchbook), 1951, esp. pp. 190-229.

CHAPTER 2

1. Not all Christians have adopted a truculent stance. Liberal Protestantism was a great historic attempt to come to terms with the Enlightenment. There have been many critics of this attempt, beginning notably with Karl Barth, who have said that it gave too much to secularity. Thomas F. O'Dea, a leading sociologist of religion, in his *Crisis of Catholicism* (Boston: Beacon, 1968) considers the *aggiornamento* of Vatican II (especially *Church in the Modern World*) to be a "second chance" for Christianity to enter into critical and meaningful dialogue with the Enlightenment.

2. It seems more helpful to call the Enlightenment thinkers "philosophes" (a French word which has passed into English) rather than "rationalists" or "encyclopedists" or "men of the Enlightenment." They were social and political writers rather than philosophers in the strict sense. They were literary men rather than scientists. ". . . 'philosophy' for them meant the ideals of the Age of Reason, of which they were the self-appointed spokesmen and ardent propagandists. They were not scientists; they did not engage in research, but they were adroit in perceiving the points at which the new science could be utilized in the attack upon traditional and authoritarian ideas about religion and society": Alan Richardson, *History Sacred and Profane*, London: SCM Press, 1964, p. 90.

3. Paul Ricoeur, *Fallible Man*, Chicago: Henry Regnery, 1965, p. xxiv.

4. Peter Gay, *The Enlightenment*, Vol. II, *The Science of Freedom*, New York: Alfred A. Knopf, 1969, p. 174.

5. Cf. E. Cassirer, *Rousseau, Kant and Goethe*, New York: Harper and Row (Harper Torchbook), 1945, pp. 1-18.

6. *Ibid.*, pp. 78, 81.

7. E. Cassirer, *The Question of Jean-Jacques Rousseau*, Bloomington: Indiana University Press, 1954, p. 27.

8. *Ibid.*, p. 76.

9. Cf. William F. Lynch, S.J., *Christ and Prometheus*, University of Notre Dame Press, 1970. He defines the modern secular project over and over as the search for innocence.

10. Rollo May, "The Innocent Murderers," *Psychology Today*, December 1972, p. 53.

11. Grundmann, "hamartano," in G. Kittel, *Theological Dictionary of the New Testament*, Grand Rapids: Wm. B. Eerdmans Publishing Co., 1964, Vol. 1, p. 305.

CHAPTER 3

1. Herbert Butterfield, *The Origins of Modern Science*, Toronto: Clarke, Irwin & Co. Ltd., 1949, p. vii.

2. Ernest Becker, *The Structure of Evil*, New York: George Braziller, 1968, p. 4.

3. Cf. *ibid.* for a moving expression of belief, despite all odds, in the scientific method and its enshrining of man's dignity, rooted in his rationality. "But a scientific theory of the causes of human ills would overcome political relativity, and compel agreement on values": p. 359.

4. H. Butterfield, *op. cit.*, p. 5.

5. This book is too short to get into the discussions about the limitations of the scientific method. Cf. Ian G. Barbour, *Issues in Science and Religion*, London: SCM Press, 1966; George W. Morgan, *The Human Predicament*, Providence: Brown University Press, 1968; Thomas S. Kuhn, *The Structure of Scientific Revolutions*, Chicago: University of Chicago Press, 1962; and especially Bernard Lonergan, *Insight*, *op. cit.*, Chapters 1-5.

6. G. Morgan, *op. cit.* p. 81; cf. pp. 82-84.

7. *Ibid.*, p. 106; cf. p. 88.

8. Blaise Pascal, *Pensées*, Penguin edition, 1966, p. 90 (Brunschvicg #72).

9. *Ibid.*, p. 95 (Brunschvicg #206).

10. Cf. P. Ricoeur, *Fallible Man*, *op. cit.*, pp. 4-8, 203-216.

11. Robert Bolt, *A Man for All Seasons*, Canadian Educational Edition, Bellhaven House: Toronto, 1963, p. 83.

CHAPTER 4

1. Cf. P. Ricoeur, *Symbolism of Evil*, *op. cit.*, pp. 309-15.

2. *Ibid.*, pp. 84, 93, 106-7, 241-43.

3. There have been some towering exceptions to this statement. Reinhold Niebuhr's life work was dedicated to exploring this complicity.

4. P. Ricoeur, *Fallible Man*, *op. cit.*, pp. xvi-xviii.

5. *Ibid.*, p. xxiii. Cf. also *Symbolism of Evil*, *op. cit.*, pp. 151-57.

6. B. Lonergan, *Insight, op. cit.,* p. 191.

7. Thomas Aquinas, *Questiones Disputae de Malo*, q. 6.

8. *Ibid.*, q. 1, a. 3.

9. B. Lonergan, *op. cit.*, p. 667.

10. *Ibid.*, p. 226.

11. My understanding of these matters relies heavily on the writings of Peter Berger, Robert Bellah and Alfred Schutz.

12. Peter L. Berger and Thomas Luckmann, *The Social Construction of Reality*, New York: Doubleday, 1966, p. 62.

13. *Ibid.*, p. 94. Cf. Bernard Lonergan, "Dimensions of Meaning," *Collection*, Montreal: Palm, 1967, pp. 253-55.

14. B. Lonergan, *op. cit.*, pp. 228-232, 688-692.

CHAPTER 5

1. The Canadian Catholic Conference of Bishops, "Sharing National Income: A Statement Issued April 12, 1972," *Catholic Mind* (October 1972), p. 59.

2. *Poverty in Canada: A Report of the Special Senate Committee*, Ottawa: Information Canada, 1971, p. xxvii.

3. Mollie Orshansky, "The Shape of Poverty in 1966," in James G. Scoville, *Perspectives on Poverty and Income Distribution*, Lexington, Mass.: D.C. Heath, 1971, p. 74. The Canadian figure is from *Poverty in Canada*, *op. cit.*, p. 11.

4. Michael Harrington, *The Other America*, New York: Macmillan, 1963.

5. N. H. Lithwick, *Urban Poverty*, Ottawa: Information Canada, 1971, p. 5.

6. Bernard F. Haley, "Changes in the Distribution of Income in the United States," in Scoville, *op. cit.*, p. 18. His figures are for 1947 and 1962.

7. *Income Distribution*, Catalogue No. 13-529, Ottawa:

Information Canada, 1969, p. 78. Their dates are 1951 and 1965.

8. *Income Distribution by Size in Canada*, Statistics Canada Catalogue No. 13-207, Ottawa: Information Canada, 1973, p. 65.

9. Mollie Orshansky, *art. cit.*, p. 82.

10. N. H. Lithwick, *op. cit.*, p. 30.

11. Joseph W. McGuire and Joseph A. Pichler, *Inequality: The Rich and Poor in America*, Belmont, Calif.: Wadsworth, 1969, p. 73.

12. Anthony Downs, *Who Are the Urban Poor?* Supplementary Paper No. 26, Committee for Economic Development, New York, 1970, p. 32.

13. David Macarov, *Incentives to Work*, San Francisco: Jossey-Bass Inc., 1970, p. 47.

14. Mollie Orshansky, *art. cit.*, pp. 80-81.

15. N. H. Lithwick, *op. cit.*, p. 30.

16. Mollie Orshansky, *art. cit.*, p. 84. Cf. *Poverty in Canada, op. cit.*, p. 12.

17. Gibson Winter, *Being Free*, New York: Macmillan, 1970, p. 27. I am heavily indebted to Gibson Winter for the approach of this chapter. Cf. his theoretical analysis in *Elements for a Social Ethic*, New York: Macmillan, 1966.

18. *Proceedings of the Special Senate Committee on Poverty*, No. 21, Ottawa: Information Canada, 1971, p. 44. Cited is the brief submitted by the Vanier Institute of the Family.

19. Cf. Howard S. Beckner, "Education and the Lower-Class Child," in A. W. and H. P. Gouldner, *Modern Sociology*, New York: Harcourt, Brace and World, Inc., 1963, p. 244.

20. Cf. Michael Dennis and Susan Fish, *Programs in Search of a Policy*, Toronto: A. M. Hakkert, 1972.

21. Proceedings of the Special Senate Committee on Poverty, No. 21, *op. cit.*, p. 50.

22. Gibson Winter, *Being Free, op. cit.*, pp. 56-57.

23. Charles Taylor, "The Agony of Economic Man," in *Essays on the Left: Essays in Honour of T.C. Douglas*, Toronto: McClelland and Stewart Ltd., 1971, pp. 228-33.